DISCOVERY OF THE LOST ART TREASURES OF CALIFORNIA'S FIRST MISSION

DISCOVERY OF THE LOST ART TREASURES OF CALIFORNIA'S FIRST MISSION

By
JAMES L. NOLAN

Commissioned by
HELEN K. COPLEY

Edited by
RICHARD F. POURADE

A COPLEY BOOK

DEDICATION

*To a Richer and Deeper
Understanding of the
California Mission Story
That Never Grows Old.*

HELEN K. COPLEY

PREVIOUS COPLEY BOOKS

The Explorers, 1960
Time of the Bells, 1961
The Silver Dons, 1963
The Glory Years, 1964
Gold in the Sun, 1965
Ancient Hunters of the Far West, 1966
The Rising Tide, 1967
The Call to California, 1968
Historic Ranchos of San Diego, 1969
Rex Brandt's San Diego, 1969
Marines of the Margarita, 1970
The Sign of the Eagle, 1970
The Colorful Butterfield Overland Stage, 1971
Anza Conquers the Desert, 1971
From Fingers to Finger Bowls, 1972
Our Historic Desert, 1973
The King's Highway in Baja California, 1974
The Cave Paintings of Baja California, 1975
The Broken Stones, 1976
City of the Dream, 1977

Library of Congress Card Number: 78-73173
ISBN: 0-913938-20-3

Foreword

The "Discovery of the Lost Art Treasures of California's First Mission" is a dramatic history of a religion as well as of the art of a missionary experience in an isolated corner of the Western World.

The story, however, began long before then, in a re-kindling of religious and exploratory fervor in Spain. Rome had acknowledged Spain and Portugal as God's best tools in the Christianizing of the Americas.

Theologians went forth with a "cosmic plan" in which primitive peoples were to become part of a new world society.

In the course of time the names of the saints of Catholicism were to be left forever on California.

The Spanish expedition of Juan Rodríguez Cabrillo made the first European exploration of the California Coast only a half century after Columbus had reached the New World. The first Christian religious ceremony in California undoubtedly was conducted at San Diego Bay in 1542, and as Cabrillo's arrival coincided with the feast day of the archangel St. Michael, the port was named San Miguel in his honor.

Three decades or so later Sir Francis Drake, the English-speaking explorer and adventurer, wintered his ship on the northern California coast. He left a name that didn't last and a vague plate of brass claiming it all for England.

A few years later, Pedro de Unamuno stopped to erect a Spanish cross on the shore of a bay that is believed to have been Morro Bay, just north of San Luis Obispo.

Within a few more years, Sebastián Rodríguez Cermeño, searching for safe havens for Spain's Manila Galleons, named an anchorage "La Baya de San Francisco," in honor of St. Francis. This probably at what was later named Drake's Bay and not the San Francisco Bay of today.

Sixty years after Cabrillo, Sebastián Vizcaíno led another formal Spanish expedition along the California Coast, bestowing new names on ports and headlands. As his own arrival at San Diego in 1602 coincided with the feast day of the Franciscan saint, St. Didacus, of Alcalá, Spain, he renamed the port as San Diego de Alcalá. Diego is the Spanish name of Didacus. Most of the names bestowed by the Cabrillo expedition disappeared from history.

The decline of Spain as an influencing power already had set in when at last the first missionaries brought Christianity to California. In 1769 — more than 200 years after the visit of Cabrillo — Father Junípero Serra and his Franciscan missionaries arrived and with them came instructions to name the first mission as San Diego de Alcalá.

So began the epic of a mission chain, stretching from San Diego in the south to Sonoma in the north, that in the view of many historians was a reflection of primitive life and lacking in any measure the religious grandeur of Colonial Mexico.

Such was not the case entirely, as revealed through the long research by the author of this book. The richness of the art treasures in the missions has not heretofore been fully appreciated. With the missionaries came the statues of the saints, or angels and archangels, and religious paintings.

The Middle Ages had long faded throughout most of the Western World but they still found expression in art as well as in the little pageants enacted in distant colonial areas. Art — and the symbolism inherent in the statues and paintings — was one means through which the Christian religion could be imparted to a native people, and also helped to keep alive for the early Spaniards and Mexicans a sense of unity with all that had been left behind.

The author, James L. Nolan, is best described as an art historian, though he is a lecturer in English at the University of California at Los Angeles, and is a research associate in California mission history with the Los Angeles County Museum of Natural History.

His research also has disclosed that in a passing of time San Diego de Alcalá, for whom the port as well as the mission had been named, was displaced as the patron saint of the settlement of San Diego, and why. In the Americanization that followed it soon became confused as to who was the patron — or patroness — of San Diego. It is a strange story, little understood until now.

The mission experience, as now seen through a sharper lens, is still, despite all that has been written and published, an unfolding drama of faith and purpose that left both a heritage for a new California and a sadness for the old.

RICHARD F. POURADE

Text Contents

Art Sections

When the Long Search Came to an End in a Desert Indian Village

Seven tall, bulky Yaqui Indians came running at me as I stood by my car taking a photo of a pleasant sunset beginning to take shape behind the small Church in the distance. I was puzzled. Rita, my wife, was at the wheel, and by the time I managed to get back into the seat, they were all about us, speaking first in Spanish, then in Yaqui. Finally someone came up to my window and shouted in English, "What are you doing taking pictures?" He was plainly furious.

I didn't answer but motioned to Rita to drive on to the little Chapel a hundred and fifty yards ahead where we hoped to find the last missing piece of art from Mission San Diego in California, here in this little Indian village in Arizona eight hours' drive from Los Angeles which we had left at sunrise. As we approached the Chapel, Rita's face became rigid, straining not to show her confusion, exhaustion, and even fear. Her periodic glances at the rear view mirror made it unnecessary for me to turn around. These men were running after us as fast as they could.

Then we saw the signs posted everywhere near the Church — $300.00 fine for photographing something. We didn't get the rest. As we reached the Church, I saw a little Indian girl playing with what looked like an old rag doll. She seemed to be talking to it as I leaned out the window. *"Dónde está el Padre, Bonita,"* I said to her, and she stood up abruptly and motioned proudly with her little hand to a trailer in back of the Church.

By the time I stepped into the Father's quarters, introduced myself, and tried to speak quickly of a large statue of the Crucifixion which I knew — no, had reason to believe — maybe better just say believe — certainly hoped was there (I don't recall what I said), the Indians were upon us or rather upon Rita outside. Somehow in the meantime they had picked up a policeman and a member of the town council. I could hear Rita's voice asking what all of this could possibly mean. As I turned toward the door, I knew she was distressed, even frightened, but it meant very little right then. I was smiling. The Padre had clearly indicated he understood and I knew a long, long search was about to end.

The difficulty was soon overcome. We were invited to attend the ceremony of *"Los Fariseos"* that night (without cameras — the point need not have been made so strenuously), and the Padre in the meantime had shown me the Crucifix of magnificent proportions and quality

1

in the Church.

As we participated in the strange ceremony that night, kneeling out in the open road holding lighted candles, underneath a white, star-filled desert sky, Indian figures looking like black outlines of life-size Katcina dolls surrounded the entire group, each silhouetted against the bright lights from the cars parked in a circle around us. Over there stood the largest Indian with a massive slip-over bear mask with vertical ears and white painted wooden pegs for ferocious teeth; over there, another with the head of a wolf; there, there, and there, the same but with grotesque humanoid masks with beady eyes — each holding either a leather braided whip or a colorfully painted sword of wood which glistened brightly in the headlights from the surrounding parked cars. Over there was the leader standing rigid and dignified, with his small round drum, looking over the candlelit group of women to our rear where Rita stood.

Still even this different, quite startling scene could not arrest my thoughts. It had been a long journey, not the one from the California coast to this little community in Arizona, but the other, from the first time I had located an important piece of missing San Diego mission art early in January of 1962. That date was on a photo I looked at just before leaving California.

Discovered over sixteen years ago, the magnificent nearly life-size statue of the Virgin in this photo stood upon a large gilded crescent moon. Unlike the last piece just found, it had not been lost physically in some distant and exotic place. It had been in the "mortuary" chapel of San Luis Rey Mission thirty-five miles north of San Diego, for years. Rather than the loss of the statue itself, its history, true origin, and identity as the patroness of both the Presidio and City of San Diego had become entirely lost for over a hundred years.

Between that time and this startling dark night in Arizona, every piece of art originally attached to the Mission up Mission Valley in San Diego had been found, except for one statue and two small paintings. In addition, the entire iconographic holdings of the Presidio Chapel of San Diego had been found as well. Together these two combined to represent the most important

collection of Spanish-American art from a single mission period community in California if not in the entire United States. But their significance far transcended that immediate value.

As I knelt there that night looking at the most striking contrasts — this little boy to my right on his knees trying to say his prayers properly and the tall stark figures behind in the shadows with their dark grotesque masks with vertical animal ears — I kept on wondering how this additional importance might be best explained to others.

Why should anyone involve himself in a sixteen-year search for the lost art of the small Presidio and Mission Churches of San Diego? Both are gone although one has been restored. The question was not intended rhetorically, and what is more had a serious answer to it. This hunt had been intermittent but long and the reasons behind it complex, in three related areas of interest. First there was the contribution this art might make to an understanding of Western man generally. Then there was the way it would contribute to our knowledge of California and San Diego life specifically. But finally there were the works of art themselves, valued not only because they constituted the most complete system of mission period art in the entire country but also because they were in themselves the most striking and beautiful.

Although each of these reasons was sufficient in itself and in fact progressed in importance throughout the sixteen-year period in the order of their presentation here (one could hardly appreciate the art for its own sake, the third reason, until it had been discovered), still the strongest motivation, there can be little doubt, was the earliest which involved the broadest implications: this rediscovery of San Diego's art could give genuine insight into the formative period of Western man in his medieval stage about which so little is known.

Still these two adobe red-tiled Churches of San Diego even as they existed in their finest hour were so small and primitive that this first point might be thought to stretch the rubber band of believability to the breaking point. But it wasn't. It was like being here participating in this ceremony in Arizona. The little boy to my right began to move around to relieve the pain caused by kneeling on the graveled road. One of the tall grotesquely masked figures standing behind me quickly came up to him and tapped him gently on the shoulder with his reata whip and straightened out his shoulders. Although no words were spoken, this fatherly message from the tall, ponderous wolf-eared figure standing so broad-shouldered high above the little boy was still plain enough: After all, you have been allowed to join the men on this holy night, separated from the women. Now act like a man. Ceremonies and art used to affect human behavior must be experienced and seen to be understood.

The desire to find the lost art of San Diego and put it back into its original order had always been based upon some such motivation. Of course, one cannot return to either the medieval or mission period in the physical sense. But what if the art survived?

Art meant something to the padres at San Diego who founded the first mission in Alta or Upper California in 1769. They knew what they were doing and understood their goals explicitly, for the political and philosophic ramifications of both Christianizing and Europeanizing the Indian wards soon to be in their charge had been set out and debated and even fought over and finally settled almost two centuries before these men began their little enterprise here in California — goals completely clarified, if not in the reign of Philip II, then certainly by the time the Franciscan Juan de Torquemada published his *Monarquía indiana* in 1615. It had been decided even then that the Christianization of such Indians in the New World would imply their Europeanization, and art would play an important role in that process.

The most extreme views regarding this matter still held staunchly today by many who persist in seeing "idols behind all altars" and essentially Indian patterns of behavior, even in many Christian beliefs, are really based historically upon 19th Century European scholarship drawn principally from the works of Jacob Grimm who seriously questioned whether the same Europeanizing process ever really went on in Europe.

But that is the very question that has become obscured by the political, philosophical, and religious revolutions of the Old World — how

was Western man originally Europeanized himself? Immediately following upon this question comes the other. How does one Europeanize anyone? The troubles encountered attempting to answer this question are enormous if dealt with in the abstract. However, here kneeling before this large white Cross with candles at its base, now the third of the fourteen that would be visited that night throughout the village, I could not help but think of one of those difficulties in a different light. If the fathers of the primitive Church were consulted, or for that matter any contemporary minister or priest concerning the central meaning of the Crucifixion, their answer would be of one accord. It would be said that God so loved the world that He gave His only begotten Son to atone for the sins of man. But here in this darkness, with the flickering wind-blown candles illuminating both the large wooden Cross and the large Crucifix now placed before it, there was an essentially different message. This Crucifix so powerfully depicting the suffering of the *Cristo* upon it said nothing to these Indians, once the fiercest of all New Spain, of what God did for man, but it and the entire ceremony which went back to their original conversion three and one half centuries ago in Sonora, Mexico, spoke only of what man did to a God-man and of what these Indians in their primitive state as men commonly did to other men. Thus this piece of art depicting the central event of the Christian faith possessed not a doctrinal but a behavioral subliminal intent. It showed not what this little boy to my right should believe but more importantly what he should and should not do. How clearly this could be seen in Arizona, but it was with shock that I recalled as I knelt there that the art form before my eyes, the Crucifix, showing Christ on the Cross, was unknown to the primitive Church and in fact did not become commonly used until the 5th Century when that growing institution in the West particularly was beginning to direct its energies to the spiritual conquest of the still barbaric nations of the north of Europe. Not in any mystic sense, this ancient process of conquest was illuminated over a millennium later and a continent and vast ocean apart by the dim candles glowing at the foot of this *Cristo* and by the entire candlelit cere-

Figures 1-2-3

The complex patterns of association lost along with much of the art in the California Missions still survive in Mexico and Spain. At the top left, opposite page, San Miguel is shown with the other archangels, as he was at the Presidio Church, directly above a Virgin on a crescent moon, in the Church of La Valenciana, Guanajuato, Mexico. Below, he is similarly seen, with San Gabriel to the left and San Rafael, to the right, on the facade of the Shrine of Ocotlán, Tlaxcala, Mexico. Above is seen the mother shrine of Our Lady of the Pillar, with permanent stars shown in relief on the marble back behind the Virgin, in the interior of the Cathedral of Nuestra Señora del Pilár, Zaragoza, Spain.

mony in Arizona.

In that darkness with the shadowy figures kneeling all about, it at first seemed patently obvious that this Cross and Crucifix in front and the grotesquely masked figures behind, represented distinct and separate cultures. And to a degree this is true. However, there are no data to suggest that the Yaqui Indians wore masks in their pagan ceremonies, over 350 years ago, while there is ample evidence which may be drawn from the apostle to the Yaqui nation himself, Padre Andrés Pérez de Ribas, to the effect "that the devil appeared [to these Indians] in the form of a dog, a coyote, toad, or snake," etc. — traditional shapes of the animalian hallucinatory deities worshipped not only by the Yaquis but by the Indians of California as well.

In other words, the grotesque masks of the figures behind, so fearsome, were not Indian art forms at all but rather devices employed undoubtedly in the first stages of the conquest to calumniate the non-Christian deities which were to be rejected. Moreover, that was their precise and consciously understood significance in the ceremony in Arizona, as explained to us by Yaqui Indians who were both devout and exceptionally well-informed about their own traditions.

The night was March 10, 1978, two Friday nights before Good Friday, two weeks before a re-enactment of the Crucifixion would take place in this small Indian village.

As I was told of this significance I was astonished to perceive that the principle involved here was first expressed over fifteen hundred years ago by St. Hilary of Poitiers, who witnessed the conversion of the Gauls in the 4th Century. This was that the present, in this case the ceremony of the *Fariseos*, was to be understood in terms of the past, and that past then used to understand the present.

The two groups were divided up, the men going before with a *Cristo*, the women following by about one hundred yards with a Virgin. The women had learned that Christ was going to be crucified, it was carefully explained to us, but the Pharisees who were behind the unholy plot, here dressed as the grotesquely masked figures surrounding the women particularly, would not allow them to inform the men. Such

was the meaning from the present to the past.

But of course the significance from the past to the present was just as obvious. The *Fariseos* here in Arizona represented the pre-Christian Indian culture in the "present" just as in the "past" they represented the pre-Christian Jewish one most unwilling to change their form of religion.

Then, the first reason for spending so much time trying to locate the lost art treasures of San Diego was the hope that this art like these ceremonies in Arizona would be a species of vestigial art that would point backward in time.

There is the independent question of the Spanish mission period culture. Historians have persisted in attempting to understand this phase of California history without paying the slightest heed to the visual art that formed one of its principal joys if not its essential character. And no better example of that neglect may be found in California than at San Diego.

When the American forces arrived there in the 1840's and the pioneer settlers in larger numbers throughout the 1850's, these strangers to Spanish-American culture encountered ceremonies in San Diego which they hesitated to call religious because they involved the entire community, not only in services in the town chapel but bull fights in the Plaza or earlier in the Presidio square, in addition to horse and sack races in the streets, concluding finally with elegant balls elaborately staged in the finest salons either in the large private homes or growing number of public ones. The most important of these, reported dutifully throughout the 1850's in the *San Diego Herald*, was called an *Aniversario*. But the Americans never understood what it was an anniversary of. The answer lay in the history of the specific art and patronage of the Presidio and Town to develop at its feet, particularly the history of the tall and gracious statue of the Immaculata whose importance to that community has been obscured now for over a century. It was in her honor that these most important ceremonies were given annually on December 8.

The difficulty existed then and remains today; this statue which in the mission period stood gloriously above the main altar of the Presidio Church remained a complete enigma to the

Anglo-American mind. Throughout mission art, as throughout the medieval world, there were two dicta employed to govern the use of art. The first conceived its function to be a book to unlettered men, held throughout the north of Europe from the time of Gregory I to Henry VIII. The large Crucifix found in Arizona but originally as late as the 1840's still at Mission San Diego, was clearly of this type. It was designed to bring forcefully to mind the horrors of the Crucifixion to those who could not read of it themselves. But the Immaculata in the Presidio Chapel, the first piece of the San Diego collection to be found and identified, just as clearly did not conform to this principle. It did not represent an historic event directly described in the gospels of any of the four Evangelists. With its strange crescent moon and star-filled halo, its meaning could only be understood with a knowledge of the doctrine of the Immaculate Conception, the teaching even more importantly of the scholastics in physics, science, and cosmology, and finally the scholastic interpretation of the last book of the New Testament, the *Apocalypse* of John from which her startling image is drawn. Furthermore, as in the *Fariseos* here too a second approach to history or time was employed wherein the statue's viewer was expected to see the present in the past and the past in the present.

Such an assertion about the meaning of this statue implied that those responsible for its use in California had to be university men in the medieval or scholastic sense of that word — knowledgeable in the doctrines of the "schools" and creative in their use of that knowledge. But, of course, that is precisely what the padres who administered the missions of California were in varying degrees, and above all the man responsible for beginning the traditions in San Diego that honored this statue of the Immaculata. For Junípero Serra taught in the "schools" of Mallorca straight out of the text of Duns Scotus and employed the entire panoply of 13th Century Aristotelian science. Without a knowledge of this, it is not possible to understand the art in the twenty-one missions of California in general and the use of the Immaculata at the Presidio Chapel of San Diego in particular. California history and the high renaissance of San Diego

life in the Spanish period have been grossly distorted by the omission of these considerations, and the attempt to fit these mission pieces into such extremely inappropriate molds of folk art rather than their appropriate vestigial forms has led not only to their misunderstanding but to their absolute neglect and eventual loss.

But fortunately, as our own experience with the *Fariseos* in Arizona, a young man from Boston, Alfred Robinson, attended a similar liturgical drama in 1829, which also took place at night in San Diego's candlelit Presidio Church which involved grotesque masks as well. With him, because of the rediscovery of this art, we will be able to kneel down in that ancient Adobe Church on Christmas Eve and vicariously experience a new understanding of these scholastic themes and comprehend their significance not only to the birth of Christ but to the birth of Christianity and European civilization certainly in California if not vestigially throughout the medieval world.

Thus the long interest taken in the lost art treasures of the San Diego Mission also related crucially to a desire to reconstruct and understand California mission period history and culture, but as that progressed and each piece was relocated over the long sixteen-year period, inevitably a third interest would develop in the art of San Diego for its own sake.

When I had left the trailer of the Padre in Arizona and stepped out into the small enclosure between it and the white stuccoed Chapel, then filled with the sound of many tongues, I unobtrusively slipped around the group and stepped into the Church where the cool, dark interior served to isolate me from the noise and the still warm but late afternoon sun outside.

Ever since the rediscovery of the Immaculata so long ago I had come to expect a high quality of workmanship in the pieces originally belonging to the San Diego mission period collection. I recalled discovering the missing eight-by-ten-foot canvas of the Day of Judgment in the small semi-private Chapel off the main sanctuary at San Luis Rey Mission. I was astonished at its quality. The Crucifix which I sought in Arizona had formerly stood before that huge painting, on the side altar to the left at San Diego Mission and later on the main altar of the small Adobe

Chapel of the Immaculate Conception in Old Town, San Diego, where it was photographed. From this view of it I expected to find an impressive work, and when I first stepped into that small Chapel in Arizona with one of these photos in my hand for comparison, my expectations were not disappointed.

The Padre turned on the spotlights which showed off this marvelously executed figure. One could look at it and understand why there was such a low rate of violent crimes in the mission period and why the same remains the case today in Spain.

Now I was ready to face the Indians, I thought. As I walked out of the Chapel, I thought how this art of the San Diego mission period had been so grossly misrepresented, not only in the inaccurate remark made of it and similar pieces elsewhere in the missions by Helen Hunt Jackson to the effect that they "were all carved by the Indians," but even in the work of contemporary and responsible scholars. It was as though this sentiment, however uncritical, simply would not die.

The Fine Arts Society of San Diego sponsored an exhibit from April 3 to May 16 in 1976 and concurrently published a catalogue of the 163 pieces exhibited entitled *The Cross and the Sword, La Cruz y la Espada San Diego 1976* with the hope that we might all "pause in the life and growth of San Diego" to gain a better understanding of "the religious and secular past of the San Diego area." In reality, although accumulated and commented upon by eminent scholars both from the San Diego area and elsewhere, this exhibit and its catalogue carried on the same uncritical preconception about the inferior quality of California mission period art.

First, none of the actual works of art from either the Mission or Presidio Churches of San Diego were included in this exhibit except a small piece showing Christ in the Garden of Gethsemane. This, of course, may not be considered an oversight, for these original works of art for the San Diego area had been lost to the eye of history for an indefinite time. However, far worse, two-thirds of the actual santos shown were unqualified species of folk art, loaned from New Mexico, Arizona, and the interior rural provinces of Mexico but hopelessly inappropriate to represent the "religious and secular past of the San Diego area."

The reason for this was perhaps most clearly explained by Jean Stern in the very publication of that exhibit, in a footnote placed at the bottom of a page in the middle of the text instead of on the first page of the catalogue:

Coastal areas in California and Texas had direct maritime access to artistic products from Mexico and Spain, and usually imported much of their religious items. By contrast, interior areas of Arizona and New Mexico [from where the greater portion of the exhibit came] were heavily dependent on locally made religious art.

It was as though the inferior pieces from the internal provinces had been selected to show the native — hopefully, if one could only prove it — pieces, to the near total exclusion of the finer types of paintings and statues found plentifully throughout the other missions of California about which much was known in 1976 when this show was put on in honor of the country's Bicentennial. This approach deprived the Spanish people of San Diego of their rightful heritage and obscured entirely the vestigial quality of that art which was of such great interest.

When I stepped out of the Chapel, I was again astonished to discover that that was exactly why the Yaqui Indians of Arizona were furious too, why they were forced to put up signs and push through local legislation to back up those signs.

Indeed, the great contribution of the anthropologists has been to point out that important vestiges of the pre-Christian Yaqui culture have survived in some significant part in the present era, but their great error has been to suggest by this that such a survival today is characteristic of present Yaqui culture. As I learned, these Indians in Arizona were aware of that survival and rejected it consciously. The irritation which they told us they felt with the "gringos from the high-class tourist magazines of the state and even from the museums" derived from the fact that these people kept on coming to these ceremonies with their elaborate photographic equipment — hence the signs — to record the events in such a way as to actually ignore or misinterpret their religious nature.

Even more irritating, year in and year out they

would come out with the same grotesque interpretations of what they saw, designed to cater to the broadest tourist appeal and even to the sentiments of the anthropologists. All of this made these Yaqui Indians appear far more barbarous than they ever did to Pérez de Ribas and his successors who first brought Christianity to that nation three and one half centuries ago. In a way the same distressing pattern has been applied to the mission period art of San Diego.

How the Long Search Began in Uncertainty and Vanished Records

On that night in Arizona, when the long search had come to an end, there also came the realization of how tenuous were the conditions under which so many objects of incalculable value had been lost and found on seas of circumstances. The principle of uncertainty challenges the art historian as well as the adventurer and entrepreneur.

Of the two great collections of Spanish-American mission art in the United States, for example, one received complete documentation by one man alone, as if by chance; the other far more sophisticated one in the twenty-one missions of California never did, no matter how many individuals tried to rectify the situation.

The earlier of these two collections, housed in the Spanish Missions of New Mexico, had a minute account drawn up of it by Fray Francisco Atanasio Domínguez, O.F.M. By the chance order of his superiors, it would seem, this careful observer visited New Mexico's distant mission outposts in 1776 and described in the most detailed manner imaginable nearly everything he saw: boards, the thickness of adobe walls, and most importantly the art, for which he gave the name, size, and exact location in the church. As a result of this one manuscript alone and its

important publication in this century, almost a complete knowledge may be had of the original art holdings of any New Mexican mission church, even if the building and its art have long since passed out of existence.

Would that the same were true of the twenty-one missions along the Pacific Coast. And how much has been lost as a consequence of this fact!

In California the very opposite occurred. Not only was there never such a document as the one compiled by Domínguez, but the steps taken by the United States in the second half of the 1840's, after the War with Mexico, eventually very nearly led to the total destruction of all extant Spanish records relating to the missionary establishments along that Western Shore. Since no single Domínguez-like manuscript existed to establish beyond doubt what did and what did not belong to a California mission, the acting military Governor, Colonel R. B. Mason, logically ordered his subordinates to watch out carefully for any such document. Therefore, on September 7, 1847, as an example, Mason's Secretary of State, H. W. Halleck, noted in a letter to the Commander of the Los Angeles area that "certain archives belonging to the mission San Luis Rey were taken to San Juan Capistrano" and then proceeded to state the government's well-intended but ultimately disastrous policy, in *California Messages and Correspondence of 1850.*

As it is desirable to collect in this office all the archives belonging to the missions of California, you are requested to use your best endeavors to procure all papers which may be likely to give information respecting their present and former condition.

So began the process.

Fatefully, these invaluable records were collected by Halleck and others and were first bound together in 1858 by Edwin M. Stanton into what eventually amounted to 289 folio volumes averaging 700 pages each. Certainly these comprised collectively the equivalent of a Domínguez document and far more. And had not uncompromising disaster struck, had these irreplaceable manuscripts only survivied — or had the two or three noted historians who employed them extensively possessed an interest in California mission art, which they did not — then the most severe problems encountered by the art historian of these institutions of California would have been easily averted. But, of course, chance chose a separate course.

Not one single text of this massive collection survives, each precious folio volume of the entire 289 having been burnt to the page in the San Francisco earthquake and fire of 1906.

Not only was the California art historian left incapable of knowing the art holdings of a mission long since passed out of existence — knowledge readily available to the historian of the New Mexican mission period art — but more frequently than he wished to admit, he was even rendered ignorant of the art holdings of many missions which survived. In an article written at the beginning of this century in *Out West Magazine,* in Volume 21, Number 3, entitled *"Old Art in California,"* for example, Charles F. Lummis, editor of the *Los Angeles Times,* claimed to have discussed "thirty-four oil paintings which hung in these Missions prior to the 'Secularization' of 1834." Because of the great loss of official records, still many, even most of these paintings may not as yet be checked against official documents from the mission period, but

a significant number of those which can (a Santa Teresa and a Mary Magdalena said to have hung in Mission San Antonio de Padua, near King City, for instance) clearly demonstrates that some if not many of these canvases referred to by Lummis really never saw the inside of a mission church in the period described. At the beginning of this century, such confusion abounded. But still there was hope.

Since Governor Mason and his subordinates lacked the most efficient means of collecting such documents, not all were found, and, ironically, therefore, not all were lost. Since the San Francisco fire, the mission archives and personal papers of important families within this state have been examined along with the great manuscript collections of Mexico and Spain. From this, a new picture began to take shape.

In some cases, it was learned, art treasures had been successfully transferred to safety. This would be only a joyous revelation except that this was often accomplished, as in most emergencies, without clear record of transfer. Many iconographic systems of exceptionally important missions have been lost, not necessarily destroyed.

The historian who had formerly committed himself to an unending search for lost documents for over three-quarters of a century now instinctively found himself looking for missing art treasures which survived the mission period. Where did these works of art go?

Of all the lonely mission establishments to have suffered most as a result of the massive loss of official Spanish records in California, none has been more the victim than the Mission and Presidio Churches of San Diego, ironically, the founding or mother institutions of the entire chain of twenty-one. Established the earliest, these two Churches were among the first to be abandoned, the Presidio Church with its art in 1842, the Mission up in Mission Valley as a religious institution and repository of its own art collection in 1848, well before any photo could be taken of their respective iconographic systems in place. As a result little has been understood of the original contents of these two historic places of worship.

No help is found from the many Anglo-American visitors to these two San Diego mission period Churches who acted as though an unknown power had sealed their lips. Alfred Robinson's account of the production of the nativity play *Los Pastores* is perhaps the only description of the interior of the Presidio Church of San Diego to come down to us in the English language (no word is spoken about its art), while the few words of Philip Crosthwaite, another early arrival, jotted down in 1848 concerning Mission San Diego — "There were ... some good oil paintings in the church" — constitute all that Anglo-American sources have to report on the art within San Diego Mission. In 1849, this art was no longer in that Church; in the 1850's the same building was turned into a barracks. A *San Diego Union* reporter, on October 3, 1870, noted that this venerable structure had long since been "divided into two floors — the upper one grave and desolate, with walls covered with rude charcoal sketches and caricatures, the lower one used principally as a stable." Three years later, on May 1, 1873, another *Union* reporter contemplating "an immense breach in the massive walls" in the northwest corner of this building complained that "unless some enthusiastic antiquarian takes in hand the preservation of this most ancient landmark of civilization in California, it will soon pass away, and be remembered among the things that were" — a cry that went unheeded for half a century. And when it was heard in the early 1930's and the building restored from the one or two walls still standing, it remained then as it still does today, merely a shell of its former existence.

In the light of this tradition of oblivion in which not a single Anglo-American from the time of Alfred Robinson in the 1820's on had identified one statue or painting by name in either of these two mission period churches of San Diego, it might have seemed hopeless to persist in a search for the present location of these missing art treasures.

But sometimes a sudden shift of the tide or of the sand of a desert may bare treasure long hidden. This is precisely what happened with regard to these two mission period churches so long disintegrated by neglect.

The recovery of some of the important official records for this area revealed not only the name of the individual works of art originally in the Mission San Diego Church up the Valley, but of course those art objects themselves as well as those from the Presidio Church have actually been found intact.

One of the key documents which made this sudden shift of circumstance possible, presently in the Santa Barbara Mission Archives, is an invaluable 1834 inventory of the effects of San Diego Mission including its art, mentioned by name and often by size, first published by Father Zephyrin Engelhardt, O.F.M., in his separate work on that Mission in 1920. Alone this text would reveal little but when compared to a large number of museum photographs taken of this art at the end of the last and the beginning of this century when it was still in the San Diego area, the entire history of San Diego's missing art is laid bare. Very simply stated, the large, imposing paintings, the delicate, hand-carved statues, and the beautifully ornate vestments were transferred from the Mission and Presidio Churches to Old Town in the 1840's and from there in the following century to four other missions of California: San Antonio de Padua near King City, San Miguel, just north of Paso Robles, San Juan Capistrano in the city of the same name, and in much greater number to San Luis Rey, from where most recently an exceptionally important piece was transferred to the small Indian community in Arizona. Due to frequent changes in personnel at these institutions, the origin of this art became completely obscured.

As already implied, no direct record was kept of this original transfer, particularly to San Luis Rey Mission, so close. Still some did remember years later. If any one individual is to be credited for bringing the historian to the last stages of the rediscovery of the lost art treasures of San Diego, that man would have to be the Reverend Dominic Gallardo, O.F.M., of San Luis Rey. After serving at that institution for over thirty years, this venerable and aged Father in the years of the 1950's took the trouble to record his own personal recollections concerning the origin of the art then at Mission San Luis Rey. This was done for a group of younger successors who would themselves initiate a virtual renaissance of historical and archaeological activities at that

Mission in the Fifties and Sixties. Thus from this single source recorded in two inventories still in San Luis Rey's historical archives, the transfer of the San Diego art to Mission San Luis Rey may be verified.

Of course, personal recollections are not in themselves proof. As one of Father Dominic's most distinguished successors, Dr. Valentine Healy, O.F.M., put it in a note to one of his unpublished manuscripts at Mission San Luis Rey, "difficulty" is certainly met "in determining what was 'original' and what not in the furnishings of the church" of San Luis Rey. It is not beyond conceivability that the art once at that Mission could have been brought to San Diego for safekeeping in the 1860's or before and then returned there in later years, as Father Dominic might be imagined saying naively, "from San Diego." The unsuspected survival of another invaluable document only recently rediscovered that clarifies this ambiguity completely is a startling testimony of the degree to which chance and circumstance still reign in the realm of research as they clearly do in other more remunerative ventures.

This manuscript contains a complete listing of the mission period art for Mission San Luis Rey, and by all rights it should have been burnt to the page with the other records in the San Francisco earthquake and fire because it had been included in the archives mentioned by Halleck taken from San Luis Rey in 1847 to Mission San Juan Capistrano (actually taken by Doña Apolinaria Lorenzana to Rancho Santa Margarita then still in the possession of the Pico brothers, according to Miss Lorenzana's own account on file at the Santa Barbara Mission Archives). Nevertheless, somehow, this important text evaded the grasp of Halleck's subordinates, and the history of its subsequent survival indeed approaches the bizarre.

Having been taken from the Pico ranch apparently to Mexico, this single leather-bound tome vanished from sight only to surface a half century later in Spain in the possession of a bookdealer. Visiting that country some ten to twenty years later, a California Father by the name of José Montañer chanced upon this very individual and picked up the invaluable text for fifteen cents. Upon his return to the West

Coast, his luck still holding, this same Padre was able to place his prize in the hands of the one man in the world most capable of appreciating it, the then already distinguished Franciscan historian of the California missions, Father Engelhardt, who, of course, immediately recognized it as the lost *Libro de Patentes* of Mission San Luis Rey. Engelhardt was astonished, but what pleased him most in the document "were the two inventories dated respectively 1808 and 1844," even calling "the Inventory of 1844 . . . especially instructive and supremely important." And yet this studied author, as was not his custom, omitted this last document entirely from his work on San Luis Rey, not even drawing a single phrase or sentence from its text. Furthermore, the same inventory seems to have eluded the eyes of scholars, certainly this one, from the day Engelhardt made reference to it in his separate work on San Luis Rey in 1921 to a time shortly before the completion of this study.

The "supreme importance" of the 1844 inventory now in the Santa Barbara Mission Archives is that it lists every mission period work of art and vestment at San Luis Rey three full years before any of these were removed by Miss Lorenzana and, therefore, completely dispells any "difficulty in determining what is 'original' and what not in the furnishing of the Church" of that Mission located so close to San Diego. But in addition to listing explicitly what was in the church and sacristy of this King of the Missions, this second document more importantly, for this study at least, also records what was not there: in this case, certain pieces of art presently at San Luis Rey which may be shown in accordance with Father Dominic Gallardo's personal recollections to have come from San Diego — as further study shows, not only from San Diego's Mission, as he said, but also from the Presidio Church of that area as well. Among this collection of San Diego's relics at San Luis Rey, incidentally, is included California's first baptismal font brought up from Lower California for San Diego by Fray Junípero Serra himself, the founder of the California Missions in 1769.

San Diego's mission period art, then, has been found. By a sudden shift of circumstance these treasured objects themselves formerly buried in the sand of the past have been revealed.

History of San Diego Mission Art and its Removal to Old Town

Mission San Diego de Alcalá was first divested of its church art under terrifying circumstances. It happened on the frightful night of November 4, 1775. A well-coordinated group of infuriated Indians from their surrounding hut villages descended upon an almost equally primitive adobe and thatch Mission, pummeled one of the two unsuspecting missionaries to death so that not a portion of his flesh was left without bloodstain or bruise, and proceeded to burn to the ground almost every building in sight. Like the small Church, the fathers' quarters and many other rooms were roofed with thatch. In no time, all was in flames.

Except for two paintings, one of the patron San Diego and another of the Virgin as Our Lady of Light, almost all else was lost to the exploding fire. Two statues, one of the Purísima Concepción and another beautiful image of San José, however, were pirated away by the retreating Indians into that terrifying blackness licked with roaring flames, leaving those still living with some hope of retrieving them later on. They were never seen again. When the soldiers brought the long-haired, broad-faced Indian leaders of the revolt back to the Presidio in irons, they were flogged "with such severity

that one of the unfortunates died. ... Nevertheless," Padre Pedro Font recorded incredulously in his diary, "it was not learned what they had done with the images of the Blessed Virgin and St. Joseph." **1**

One of the exceptionally stoic members of this band, ignoring the personal and repeated pleas of Fray Junípero Serra, actually strangled himself to death with a makeshift cord in San Diego's Presidio prison, **2** and with him died any hope of regaining the lost treasures.

Such were the gruesome circumstances surrounding San Diego's first dispossession. Until very recently, that unfortunate Mission's second loss of its entire iconographic holdings, which vanished mysteriously from the eye of history in the middle of the last and again at the beginning of this century, seemed equally complete and final. For Time itself, like those confused but resolute Indian leaders of the 1775 uprising, seemed to prefer an imprisoned silence, refusing steadfastly to reveal the location of the Mission and Presidio art treasures. And the more one reads about the gradual ruin of the only two Churches of the San Diego area in the mission period, the more deeply does one feel the mystery of this disappearance.

In the 1820's in San Diego, when the *inválidos* or retired soldiers were beginning to build small adobe houses down the hill from the Presidio, **3** in what is now called Old Town, there were only two Churches in the immediate vicinity, one at San Diego Mission several miles up the Valley and the other more convenient to the settlers of the town, atop Presidio Hill. The latter, located within fortified walls yet not exactly within a fort, and also identified as the Chapel for the Port of San Diego, fell into ruin well before the one at the Mission. According to José Antonio Pico in a letter to Mariano Guadalupe Vallejo, once military *comandante* in the north, by 1839, "except for the Church, not a building was left standing in the old Presidio." **4** However, even this ecclesiastical structure was probably last used only two years later, late in 1841 when the new bishop, the Reverend Fray García Diego y Moreno, "administered the Sacrament of confirmation to 125 persons in the presidio chapel" on December 18. **5** Eight years later, this building whose ground plan, main altar, side chapel, and baptistry have only recently been excavated, was in complete ruin, certainly by 1849 when Henry Delano Fitch, a Massachusetts-born merchant, was buried there. **6**

This precipitous decline of the Presidio along with its historic Church in the late Thirties and early Forties has been attributed to the excessive poverty of the district *comandante,* who is asserted to have sold the tiles even off the roof of the *iglesia* to pay his own salary, while others have blamed the Americans. E. W. Morse remarked in his reminiscences that "the roofing tiles and most of the adobes and other building materials [there] had been utilized in building up the new town on the flat," and "it was not long ... before even the Church walls were carried away, probably by some undevout 'gringo'." **7** Whoever was to blame, one cannot easily understand how this dismantling of the Presidio Church could have taken place if the obvious religious needs of the residents of Old Town on the southern flat had not been met in some other way. Yet, if what happened to the entire Presidio, to say nothing of one of its principal buildings, its Church, remains somewhat a mystery, certainly so too does the disappearance of this most historic Presidio Chapel's

works of art. The most likely conjecture would be that they were taken to the only other Church then in the vicinity, the one at the Mission several miles up the Valley; however, there is no record of such a transference, and such a solution would have still left the residents of Old Town without religious accommodations of any kind.

So went the Presidio Church, then. It was put to rest perhaps in 1842. However, twelve years later, by 1854, after the American conquest, the San Diego Mission Church was itself being used as a barracks, **8** and one has to pay the closest attention to the documents of the period to get any idea of the activities there at the Mission between the last baptismal entry in June of 1846 and the later military occupation of the Church in 1854. If this is done carefully, some clues to the subsequent location of the entire Mission's art treasures then presumably added to by the effects of the Presidio Church begin to appear. But these annoyingly remain at best only clues.

Archibald H. Gillespie, a Marine Corps captain commanding the volunteer forces of California in the District of San Diego, "visited the mission in August 1846 and was there shown by Padre Oliva a large square of houses and a corral, a house for the padre and one for the servants and working people, several storehouses and offices, and a large church with ancient and rich ornaments." **9**

In August of 1846, then, San Diego Mission was still in possession of its Church art. However, as Gillespie continued to point out in summary, "from August 1846 until long after the war was over troops of the Regular Army, volunteers, and Marines under Kearny, Stockton, Stephenson, and R. B. Mason were quartered there, and that much of the perishable property [not the art] was appropriated and made use of by the United States." **10**

At the beginning of this period of occupation, Padre Vicente Oliva, the last Franciscan at San Diego, retired to Mission San Juan Capistrano in 1846, leaving a life of memories behind. It was he who had celebrated midnight Mass in 1829 just before the famous production of the *Pastores* directed by Don José Estudillo. Now he would depart leaving this old friend and director of the *Pastores,* Don José, in charge of the Mission. Yet two conflicting claims to the

Mission properties would be presented to the United States Forces, nevertheless. While Gillespie was still at San Diego in 1846, "Don Santiago Argüello ... placed in his hands papers and documents in relationship to his right and proprietorship to the mission" based upon its sale to him by Pio Pico. 11 On the other hand, "Fr. Oliva ... named José Antonio Estudillo administrator of Mission San Diego." 12 Estudillo was one of the most aristocratic of Spanish settlers and remained aloof during the war.

Daniel C. Davis, Captain, First Company, of the famed Mormon Volunteers (the first to take up quarters at the Mission itself but not as yet in the Church) also took note of this complex legal circumstance upon his arrival there in 1847. In his October 17 letter addressed to Colonel J. D. Stevenson in that year, he remarked that "the occupant of the Mission states he was left in charge of the Mission and property in August, 1846, by Fr. Vicente Oliva, now residing at Mission San Juan Capistrano. A power of attorney from said Fr. Oliva to José A. Estudillo shows he still claims jurisdiction of the property. [However] Santiago Argüello has also a claim, purporting to be a sale to him of the Mission by Pio Pico when he was governor of California." 13

Included in the Davis letter was a copy of the Pio Pico bill of sale, which clearly exempted from the entire transaction, according to its fourth article, "the Church and all pertaining thereto and the residence of the officiating priest." 14 This meant, even if the Argüello claim had been recognized, which it had not been in accordance with "the best information then [available] upon California affairs" regarding its legality, 15 that his suit would not have pertained to the property of the Mission Church. Therefore, José Antonio Estudillo's role as the legal guardian of the art in that Church would have gone and undoubtedly did go uncontested. Moreover, it is this same Estudillo who is found actively concerning himself about the valuables in the Church during the first years of the American occupation when such attention apparently was needed.

While residing at San Juan Capistrano in 1848, Father Oliva's successor, Fray José Joaquín Jimeno, received a letter from this Don José Estudillo, certainly the de facto guardian of the Church properties. It had been made clear to the Padre previously that "the doors of the Church of Mission San Diego have been removed; and that from the wardrobes, in which the sacred vessels and other valuables usually adorning the altar were preserved, they took out chalices and silver candlesticks." 16 Don José Estudillo had found most of these items in a net in the sand of the adjacent arroyo: "one silver ciborium, three chalices, two pieces of silver the purpose of which I do not know, two silver candlesticks, etc." As Father Jimeno had been informed in the other letter, some of these items had been "found in the smithy of the Americans, already broken to pieces." Apparently even the gilded wooden tabernacle of the Church, received in 1779, was missing. As a consequence of this intelligence, Father/President Jimeno, in conjunction with Apolinaria Lorenzana, "determined to bring away all the vestments and valuables of said church." 17 Apolinaria Lorenzana, who had been sent to California from Mexico as a foundling, became known as *La Beata*, the pious.

San Diego's art treasures, then, were not destroyed heedlessly either by the Spanish or American residents of San Diego, nor were the statues used for target practice as was said to have happened at other missions. 18 They were cautiously removed from the Mission Church in the year 1848, as is testified to by an inventory made of the movable goods at the Mission in that year, 19 at a time when those works of art were still in a good state of preservation. This fact is confirmed by Philip Crosthwaite, who upon leasing the mission from Colonel J. D. Stevenson in October of 1848, "removed there with his family to the priest's house" and reported in that year that "with few exceptions the old rooms, offices, and workshops were then in good order. ... He found there many trunks full of priests' clothing. There were rich vestments, chalices, and various church furniture, some good oil paintings in the church." 20 In 1849, Crosthwaite reported, all of these invaluable treasures had been removed. 21 The only question was, where?

Without these sacred objects, the Mission Church became once again a mere building, a condition given quasi-official status eventually by Father J. C. Holbein, San Diego City's new and first resident priest, when he removed the bones of three Franciscans from the Mission Church's sanctuary on December 27, 1853, and placed them in the Mission cemetery. **22** In November of that year, plans had already been made to renovate this Church building which the editor of the San Diego *Herald* euphemistically styled "Improvements at the Mission:"

It is contemplated to repair part at least, of the old Mission Church, so as to provide Hospital accommodations for the sick, a school room, and a chapel for Divine worship. When these improvements are all completed, no Military Post in the United States will present a more pleasing aspect than this.

What actually happened as opposed to what was merely planned was succinctly reported in the journal of Lieutenant David Sloan Stanley of the Second U.S. Dragoons, who accompanied Lieutenant A. W. Whipple on his survey for a railroad route to the Pacific in 1853: "The church is being converted into barracks for soldiers." **23** This apparently is how the building is shown in the earliest photos. Four years later, editor John Judson Ames of the San Diego *Herald* visited the Mission in October of 1857 and was not then so sure all was improvement. Looking about him, he sadly recalled that here "had dwelt a thriving and happy population of christianized Indians" whereas on the day of his visit "all looked deserted and ... crumbling to decay." Even "the place in the Church where once stood the Altar ... is now occupied by 'grim-visaged men of war'," he complained. Certainly nothing remained of the Mission's art, not even the bells: "the church-going bells which once called the natives to the house of prayer, have been removed from the belfry and now adorn a gallows erected in a corral near the Plaza, and the cross — that sacred emblem consecrated to this temple of the Most High — has been taken down and cut up to light the evening camp fires" of the soldiers. **24** So went the foundation Cross of Mission San Diego de Alcalá. **25**

Surely where these "church-going" bells went, so too would go the religious art of the Mission, for their function was to call the entire community to the place of worship that housed that art. Most significantly, later residents of Old Town would recall that such "a bell frame stood on the adobe wall at the rear of the courtyard" of the house belonging to the same man to whom Father Oliva had given legal custody of the Mission properties, including certainly the Church art, Don José Antonio Estudillo. "An alley ran between this wall and the one opposite belonging to the Altamirano home, from San Diego Avenue to Couts Street." **26** Other "'Old-timers' also recalled" more specifically "that seven bells from the ruined Mission once hung in this [Estudillo] courtyard on wooden beams bedded in a pierced adobe wall." **27**

All evidence, direct and indirect, suggests, then, that the vestments, chalices, candlesticks, and other valuables of the Mission Church including its art, were not lost but carefully transferred to the Estudillo House. Therefore, it is not in the least surprising to discover in September of 1851 the first well-known public ceremony of a religious nature in Old Town — involving the use of richly-laden vestments obviously from the Mission — emanating from that important mansion located at the east end of the plaza, an entourage coming from the Estudillo House intent upon the formal laying of a cornerstone for this tiny community's first church:

At 4 o'clock precisely, the folding doors of a large apartment in the house of Don José Antonio Estudillo, used for private worship, were thrown open, and a procession composed of the most esteemed and cherished members of the Church Universal, with the learned and devout "Padre" [Holbein] in full canonicals at their head, preceded by interesting youths dressed in snow white frocks and bearing in their hands silver vases and gold and silver candlesticks of great length, issued into the Plaza, and was increased every moment by the addition of citizens ... until it reached the sacred spot. In the center of the area already marked out in the form of a large parallelogram, was placed a table richly ornamented with solemn ecclesiastical devices, and covered with cloths of the richest fabric. The never-failing emblem of the sins of man and the atonement by the crucifixion of our Divine Saviour, occupied a conspicuous place, towards which the procession slowly wended its way with solemn chants. A circle being formed ..., the prayers being over, the priest consecrated with holy water the foundations of the building; after which, a scroll containing a memorandum of the date and place ..., together with the names of several who formed a part of the procession, was securely sealed in a vessel of indestructable (sic) nature, and placed under the cornerstone about to be laid. **28**

This "large apartment," this "great hall in which it was customary to hold the services of the Church" **29** from which this procession emanated was located according to a later account "in the northwest (sic) corner of the Estudillo House [and] was originally two rooms. The corner room was the reception room [with] a door opening into San Diego Avenue. A partition with a door through the center divided this room from a much larger inner room." **30** The large compartment to the right of the main entrance, on a plan drawn by Hazel Wood Waterman, had a temporary partition just as described above and a door facing onto San Diego Avenue, across the street from which was placed the peal of Mission bells next to the courthouse at times when the Estudillo House did not have its corral. **31**

The dimensions of this larger inner room were approximately twenty by forty feet with a twelve-foot ceiling, as a member of the family and resident of the Estudillo House, Victoria Pedrorena Magee, who taught school there in the early Sixties, **32** recorded on an official school report for the City of San Diego. Her receipts and the city's monthly payments to Mrs. Estudillo for the use of the compartment as a school are still on file at the Serra Museum in San Diego. This hall, then, comparable in size to, if not larger than the Church which would later be provided for the community and known as the Adobe Chapel (dimensions: approximately thirty-five feet long, fifteen feet wide, twelve feet high at the eaves and sixteen feet at the ridge of the roof), was certainly sufficient in size to receive all of the art from Mission San Diego, including the painting of the Last Judgment which was, according to the 1834 inventory, over eight feet tall. **33**

The art that had meant so much to the padres and the Indians from the Mission, then, was surely transferred to this compartment in the Estudillo House, to the home of the man who had legal custody of it, and then would have been placed in the Church whose cornerstone had been laid according to the above *Herald* report on September 29, 1851, in lot one of block eighty-eight according to Lieutenant Cave Johnson Couts' map of Old Town then on file with the City officials. **34** This would have been done, that is, except that though it was dedicated in 1851 with such ceremony, it was probably never really completed, **35** making the compartment in the Estudillo House the probable repository of the Mission art throughout this entire period, although this matter is still not entirely clear.

This view is exactly confirmed by Circuit Judge Benjamin Hayes, who noted in his journal in September, 1856:

For some time Rumor has had it that Don José Aguírre had made a vow ... to build a Catholic Church. There is none here now, mass being said, when a priest casually arrives, in a large room in the house of the Estudillo family. **36**

If finished at all, the Church deeded in 1850 **37** and dedicated in 1851 could have been used only for a brief period in 1854, at which time visiting Fathers from San Luis Rey and San Juan Capistrano consistently referred to their religious accommodations at San Diego as a chapel. **38** For the year 1856 and "for some time" before that, Judge Hayes, a practicing Catholic who would have known, placed the matter beyond doubt. This point is important because on New Year's night of 1855 heavy rains undermined this 1851 Church's north wall which "fell with a crack that could be heard all over town." **39** If the Church were in use and the Mission art in it, surely some would have been lost or damaged. However, nothing of this sort was reported either then or later on by citizens who lived within a few blocks of these buildings all their lives and who took an interest in these matters.

Francis Hinton Whaley, **40** the eldest child of the pioneer Thomas Whaley, even more than his father saw an era passing away before his eyes and tried ingeniously to arrest it on glass plates using an engraving process still not understood. He took views of some of the principal houses of Old Town and made a set of the entire Mission chain. The latter has been lost. He tells us specifically in a fourteen-page handwritten document now in the Whaley House in Old

Town that "prior to the use of the adobe building [on Conde Street] for religious purposes, the chapel or church of the town was at the old Estudillo home. ... After the abandonment of the old Mission of San Diego and about the time of its occupancy by U. S. troops ..., the trappings, old pictures, statuary and other altar decorations were moved from the Mission to a little adobe building just to the east of the old Bandini home ..., and there was maintained the Church of Old Town for [a] period of time." Whaley added that this house had completely disappeared from view. "After which the old chapel in the Estudillo home ... was secured and up to the early [sic: actually late] 1850's was used for church purposes." Although somewhat inaccurate with respect to time, the statement about the adobe building "just to the east of the old Bandini home" is entirely new and could refer to the Church begun on block eighty-eight in 1851 which according to Couts' map was four blocks east of the Bandini and Estudillo homes.

After interviewing such people, Hazel Waterman, who oversaw the restoration of the Estudillo House in 1910, stated matter of factly in her unpublished report entitled *The Restoration of a Landmark (Casa Estudillo)* now in the Serra Museum, that the "treasures from the first California Mission were brought to the Estudillo house for safe keeping." [41] Careful investigation shows the fundamental soundness of that assertion, since we have seen the dedicatory procession emanating from the Estudillo House in 1851 according to the *Herald*'s report, have heard so many visitors remark as late as 1853 that the town chapel was still located in a private residence, and have heard Judge Hayes identify that Chapel in 1856 as the one in the Estudillo House. Thus when Hazel Waterman noted as she did again on page seven of her report even more specifically that "after the secularization of the mission by Mexico, images and other sacred relics were brought here [to the Estudillo House] for safe keeping, and one room in the house was used as a chapel," it must be realized that such statements had been gleaned from local residents who were keenly aware of their responsibility to pass this information on to future generations. Yet however strong a tradition, such reports may not as yet be considered proof.

Matters became more reliable regarding the transfer of these objects from the Estudillo House to the new Adobe Chapel of the Immaculate Conception on Conde Street. Francis Whaley reported that "when that good hearted, noble man, Señor Don Aguirre came to the front and gave to the Catholic Church the present little chapel they did again move quarters into it and from that time until the present it has been the only church that Old Town has been able to possess. There hang the old Mission bells ..., while inside are the old mission pictures, statuary, altar-decorations, and the old baptismal font said to be used by Father Serra when in charge of the Mission of San Diego. ..." [42] Nothing was mentioned of any loss from the heavy rains of 1855. Furthermore, the vestments from the Mission were placed there as well, as Lillian, Francis Whaley's younger sister, took the trouble to note in her *Memoirs*: "A famous old chest stands in the North wing [i. e., in the addition closest to Conde Street] in which are kept the priest's robes, the altar linen and other accessories." [43]

The dedication of this modest Church, formerly the home of Captain John Brown [44] and according to Francis Whaley subsequently "a saloon and a bowling alley," was nevertheless accomplished with the greatest ceremony. Very likely there was again a procession from the Estudillo chapel, although no report of it survives. A full honor guard from the military post, as of old at the foundation of important missions, fired salvos repeatedly throughout the ceremony. "After Mass they partook of a splendid dinner prepared for them at the house of Don José Antonio Aguirre." [45] Nothing was said about Mission art in the small article covering the dedication in the *Herald*'s November 27, 1858, issue; however, the first description of this art was given in the same column and page in an article covering a bizarre case of vandalism: "On Saturday night last," two days before the dedication on Monday, "a citizen of the town, while under the effects of some of the Minnie Whiskey sold about the place, broke into the new Catholic Church and caused some considerable damage by breaking the candlesticks, wax images, and the crucifix. When found he was mounted on the top of the altar, embracing a figure of Christ on the Cross, which is very large, franticly (sic) imploring him to hear, and in his delirium he had broken off the arms and otherwise disfigured the body." **46**

This important passage is the first concrete contemporary evidence to support the very strong local tradition that the art within this Church in fact did constitute the lost art treasures of the Mission of San Diego, formerly housed in the Estudillo House. For San Diego Mission Church certainly did possess just such a *Cristo Grande* of near life-size proportions as mentioned in its 1834 inventory. **47** These local traditions recorded by so many authors and this one concrete description of a Passion-size Crucifix certainly warrant a thorough investigation of all photos known to have been taken of the interior of this little Adobe Chapel in Old Town San Diego, especially those that can be dated before or around the turn of the century, now scattered throughout many photographic archives in California.

But before this is done, a point must be made about the iconographic development of the first Mission founded in California in relationship to the social life of the Spanish-American community of Old Town in the last century. It relates to the patronage of this little Adobe Chapel, *"dedicada a la Inmaculada Concepción."* **48** That also was the title given to the later Church, originally begun by Father Antonio Ubach in 1869 in commemoration of the centennial of the Mission and City's foundation but not completed until 1917. Such was the designation of the bells of the Mission Church. Even the first baptisms after the 1775 revolt were performed on December 8, the feast of the Immaculate Conception, in 1777. More significantly, the only iconographic fact known with certainty about San Diego's Presidio Chapel was that a statue of the Immaculate Conception was provided for it in 1790. And finally, if one reads through the nine years of the San Diego *Herald* carefully, he will discover not only that December 8, the feast of the Immaculate Conception, was by far the most important fiesta in Old Town during the Spanish period, but also that the Virgin in this presentment is referred to again and again as the patroness of the city. On December 10, 1853, editor Ames of the *Herald* made the following report upon this local custom:

Every year the natives [Spanish Americans] of the country round San Diego are wont to celebrate ... the coming of the anniversary known as the Fiesta of the Patrona. It is a sort of religious affair, and is piously observed by services in the church, bull fights in the Plaza, and balls in the evening. ... Beginning on the 8th of December, the Fiesta will not be concluded until the 25th, at Christmas. ... The great feature of the festival was a *baile* or ball given in the evening [of December 8, the feast of the Immaculate Conception], one of the invitations to which was couched in the following terms:

BAILE ANIVERSARIO
dado en celebridad de la Patrona de San Diego
— 000 —
Nosotros los abajo firmada, respetuosamente suplicamos a V. y su familia para que se sirvan asistir a una
REUNION SOCIAL
Que tendrs' efecto en la Casa nombrada Gila, en San Diego, el Jueves procisimo, 8 de Deciembre 1853, a las 8 de la noche. **49**

This night was a splendid occasion, never to be forgotten by Anna Eloise Whaley who arrived in San Diego with her husband on that very day only to be swept away to this gala function at the Gila House on that evening. In the salon where the ball was held, she recalled,

the windows and doors stood open and formed frames for dark faces and graceful figures, the women in loose dress and bright shawls ..., the men wearing wide-brimmed, high crowned hats, short jackets and button bedecked pantaloons ..., the men ... in conventional black, the ladies in heavy, rich brocade silks, with very wide skirts. ... The musicians were Spanish, the instruments guitars, violins and accordians. From time to time the musicians while playing would direct complimentary remarks to the señoritas upon their dancing, dress, tiny feet, and pretty faces. ... [When a] caballero knelt before a lady clapping his hands, she [would rise], make a few graceful turns in the center of the room and return to her seat unless the caballero insisted upon having her dance which he indicated by placing himself in the way whenever she essayed to return to her seat. Every lady in the room was called upon and expected to respond to the compliment and though the shyer ones sometimes refused to rise at first, they were glad to finally rid themselves of the persistent, kneeling, clapping, teasing caballero.

As the night wore on few would recall the

occasion of the fiesta given in honor of the Immaculata.

To the music of a slow waltz the couples [would] move about and as two couples [would] approach each other, they [would] form, still dancing, into any one of the numerous figures of the contradanza ..., a beautiful kaleidoscope of swaying, bowing forms and swinging arms and rhythmically moving feet. ... [That night] a lady ... glided around the room, keeping time with the music by a peculiar, shuffling of the feet and clacking of the heels upon the floor. A tumbler of water was placed on the head, not a drop of which was spilled. ... She was clapped and cheered enthusiastically while gold and silver pieces and little bags of gold dust were flung at her feet. ... The brilliant scene stamped itself indelibly upon [the] memory. **50**

Probably the most conspicious man standing in the Gila House ballroom on that evening was John Judson Ames, a giant in stature. In his *Herald* article containing the invitation, he gave some attention to the ball itself: "All the beauty and gallantry that San Diego can furnish was fully represented," **51** etc., but did not forget the significance of the entire affair since his report was captioned *"The Grand Fiesta of the Patron Saint"* of the City of San Diego, by which he meant, as he stated the previous year, *El Fiesta Virgine (sic)*. In 1852, he spelled it out: "Wednesday next the 8th ... is the feast of the Conception of the Virgin Mary. ... This day will be set apart by the native Californians as one of general rejoicing and merry making. Great preparations are making in old town, to celebrate this day in an appropriate manner; the whole of the Plaza has been fenced in for the purpose of having a Bull Fight in the afternoon as soon as the Church ceremonies are completed; the whole will conclude with a social Ball, to be given [that year] at the house of Don Juan Bandini. ..."

H. M. T. Powell found himself in San Diego on December 8, three years earlier, in 1849, and wrote in his journal for that day and month: "Lounging around. ... The Public Square is boarded in for a bull fight; miserable affair." **52** Anna Eloise Whaley had a similar reaction in 1853 when watching the spectacle from "the upper veranda of the Colorado House overlooking the Plaza. ... The bulls were brought in. A mad rush followed, not only in the ring but on the veranda. The number of spectators had been reduced by one." Mrs. Whaley "had beat an instant and decided retreat" and "never attended another bullfight." **53**

Any historian of the Southwest would recognize the features of these familiar events for what they were said to be, the traditional fiesta given in honor of the patron of a particular Spanish-American community. Time deadening all, as the years and decades passed, few would recall this fact, with some noted exceptions. Forty years after this 1853 ball given in the Gila House, Anna Whaley's daughter Lillian would remember well in 1893 when celebrating this feast on December 8 for that year. She did not witness the customary bullfight in the Plaza, for it "had passed entirely out of date as a part of the festivities of a modern 8th of December celebration" for "the Feast of the Immaculate Conception or Virgin's Day." But the traditions lingered on down at the Old Adobe Chapel.

There in 1893, Lillian Whaley saw something "high in the center of the altar," not the large Crucifix but a "Madonna robed in soft white and blue satin [the colors of the Immaculata]. The clasped hands, over which a golden bracelet was slipped many years ago by a devout worshipper, held a bouquet of flowers. The crescent curved at her feet. The face is sweet, simple, mild, and on the head rests the high, branching golden crown surmounted where the branches meet in the centre by a small globe or cross. The altar was a bank of flowers. ... Tall candlesticks holding lighted candles which shone softly and steadily were arranged regularly amidst the flowers." **54** What was this image? Or more importantly, where did it come from?

Even more than this, one central question must present itself to anyone only remotely interested in the history of the San Diego Old Town community: Why was this yearly fiesta given in honor of the Immaculate Conception? Why not San Diego de Alcalá? That was the name of the town, Presidio and Mission to develop there. At first the editor of the *Herald* thought this December 8 celebration simply "a time honored custom in all Catholic countries." **55** However, he later learned that although his first assumption was true to some degree, it was not true absolutely. For he wrote, "the annual fiesta in honor of the

Patron Saint of the Mission" San Luis Rey took place with these similar events happening among equally "large numbers of all classes assembled. ... As has been the custom in former years," he continued to write, "various religious exercises took place in the chapel of the Mission [of San Luis Rey], followed by the usual amusements of bull-fighting, horse-racing, dancing, etc." **56** These events at San Luis Rey, however, did not begin on December 8 as in San Diego but on August 25, on the feast day of the patron of that community. In Los Angeles even farther to the north, they were held on August 2.

The question of interest, of course, is why wasn't this annual celebration in Old Town San Diego held on November 12 when the Franciscans customarily honor San Diego? In order to understand this interesting tradition in the small Spanish-American community which developed at the foot of Presidio Hill, which honored the Immaculata instead of San Diego de Alcalá, a careful investigator must turn the pages of California history back to the very beginning of the conquest of Alta California to the year 1769 and follow unblinkingly the iconographic development of that community. Only then will he gain some appreciation of the importance of the graceful statue of the Immaculate Conception seen by Lillian Whaley above the main altar of San Diego's Adobe Chapel in Old Town on December 8, 1893.

Who Was the Patron Saint of San Diego? Mystery Is Solved

On August 19, 1778, in a letter addressed to Reverend Rafael Verger, Fray Junípero Serra, the founder of the California missions, recalled the prepartions made in Lower California for the foundation of three new missions, San Diego in the south, Monterey in the north, and San Buenaventura in the center of Upper California.

"More than nine years ago, in company with Father Parrón, at the Port of La Paz, and in the presence of the Most Illustrious Señor Gálvez, I myself, with my own hands, picked out this material, piece by piece." **57** These selections of art objects and vestments, Serra later noted, were divided into "three equal parts" and packed "in three large boxes of China ... to furnish the three missions: San Carlos, San Buenaventura on the channel, and San Diego of the Port." **58**

Naturally, everything selected was carefully inventoried and these lists later included in Fray Francisco Palóu's *Noticias de la Nueva California.* **59** Among these articles were included just three altar-size images of the Virgin. There were two statues, a Virgin and Child known as Nuestra Señora de Belén, supplied to the expedition by the Archibishop of Mexico,

the Reverend Francisco de Lorenzana, through Don Joseph Gálvez, and "una imagen de la Purísima Concepción, de vara y media de alto." **60** California Historian Herbert E. Bolton correctly called this second statue, taken from the Mission "del Pilár" or "Todos Santos," an Immaculate Conception. The third image brought to New California in 1769 was a painting: *"un lienzo grande de Nuestra Señora de los Dolores"* **61** taken from a mission of the same name. Therefore, a Virgin and Child (the Belén), an Immaculata, and a Dolores were brought to Upper California in 1769, but how were they employed?

Serra tells us of his use of the Belén, that is, of the Virgin and Child known as the Conquistadora both at San Diego in the first year and later at San Carlos up north; it was placed upon the foundation altar at the first mission site in Alta California on Presidio Hill in San Diego in 1769 and kept there on that altar until the expedition turned northward for the second time to found San Carlos in Monterey. "The holy image," Serra recalled in Monterey shortly after the foundation of Mission San Carlos de Borromeo, had "occupied earlier for the space of almost a year the altar of the Mission San Diego, attending as many Masses, high and low, as were celebrated, not to mention the daily prayers, morning and evening, of the poor Indians." **62**

This statue of the Belén, as generally, may have been shown breast feeding the Infant in her arms, which may have been why the pagan Indian women of the San Diego area in that first year were inspired to thrust their breasts through the poles of the Mission stockade on Presidio Hill to show their willingness to feed that tiny Infant too. **63**

But which of the two altar-size images brought from Lower California still remaining did Serra leave behind him for the main altar of San Diego when he took this Virgin and Child northward to Monterey, the large painting of the Dolores or the statue of the Immaculate Conception?

The answer to this question is crucial to an understanding of the iconographic development of the San Diego community. If the Immaculata had been left behind, then that might explain in part why she and not San Diego de Alcalá, the patron of the Mission San Diego, became the Patrona of the Presidio and City and why subsequently the Churches built in Old Town San Diego and the most important annual fiesta given there were all named in her honor.

Serra himself does not state which of these two remaining images of the Virgin was left behind at San Diego in 1770. Neither does his biographer Fray Francisco Palóu or the official records of Mission San Diego. Unfortunately when the annual reports started in 1774, they were not inventories of everything then in the Church but only annual accounts of materials received each year. They did not tell retrospectively what had been at the Mission from the start.

By 1783, when San Diego Mission had its first complete inventory drawn up, the revolt of 1775 had already taken place and therefore information was omitted concerning the image of the Virgin left by Serra because it had been taken by the Indians eight years before never to be seen again. What was her title? We are informed of this fact in just a single source, *The Complete Diary of Pedro Font.* When at San Gabriel on November 5, 1775, Fray Pedro Font heard of the uprising in San Diego and went there accompanied by Captain Juan Bautista de Anza,

where the observant Father recorded that two statues were taken by the Indians, one of "la Purísima Concepción" and the other of "Sr. San Joseph." **64**

The statue left behind by Serra in 1770, therefore, was an Immaculate Conception. It was over four feet tall, and it remained the principal icon at the original Mission site on Presidio Hill from 1770 to 1774 when the Mission was moved up the Valley. In this four-year period, moreover, this imposing statue of the Virgin was unquestionably the principal image of the Mission-Presidio Church, which possessed at that time only a small painting of San Diego de Alcalá. **65** Furthermore, if not at this time then certainly later, this statue came to be known as the patroness of the entire military establishment at San Diego.

These observations and their implications are confirmed precisely in the *Memorias de Doña Apolinaria Lorenzana* taken down by Tomás Savage in Santa Barbara in May of 1878 and now in the Bancroft Library of the University of California at Berkeley. This testimony is of particular reliance because it was taken from the lips of a woman who had waited hand and foot upon the statues in San Diego in her youth in both the Presidio and Mission Churches and who was ultimately responsible for bringing that art from the abandoned Mission in 1848 to Old Town. Apolinaria Lorenzana recalled thirty years after those events transpired what may be inferred by a careful analysis of San Diego's iconographic history, that *"la patrona de los militares en San Diego era la Purísima Concepción."*

As a result, the lost Immaculata at the new Mission site up the Valley was never replaced after it was stolen, while at the Presidio, a new image of appropriate dignity was furnished as soon as possible, certainly by February 10, 1790, when Lieutenant José de Zúñiga "had the pleasure of informing" his mother "that in the course of the past year a beautiful church had been commenced at the presidio under his charge and an image of the pure and immaculate conception provided for it." **66** In 1842 when the Presidio Church went to ruin, this Virgin more than likely was transferred to the Mission of San Diego by Apolinaria Lorenzana, although no record survives to attest to that fact, just as it along with the rest of the Mission Church furnishings was brought to Old Town six years later by the same woman and placed in the Estudillo House, from where it was transferred ten years later in 1858 to the Old Adobe Chapel on Conde Street named in its honor. There the very same image was described by Lillian Whaley clothed in "soft white and blue satin" standing on the altar in the center of "a bank of flowers" and "tall candlesticks" with "the crescent curved at her feet."

The sequence of these events, the placing of the Immaculate Conception on the altar of the Mission-Presidio at San Diego in 1770 by Serra himself, the maintenance of such an image there in the Church at the military installation on the hill and later in the small community to develop on the southern flat just at the foot of Presidio Hill, the establishment there in her honor of the *aniversario* celebrations on her day, December 8, with all the attendant activities appropriate to a patrona of such a community, the express statements made to that effect that this Immaculata was indeed just such a patroness of the City of San Diego both by Lorenzana and editor Ames, and finally the naming of the churches built in that small community in her honor, all lead one to conclude that the Mission and the Presidio-City developed along clearly distinct iconographic lines which were later merged and confused by historians.

This point is made even more clear when the 1834 inventory of the Mission, which included even peso valuations, is examined carefully. The principal image honored was the statue of the patron, placed directly above the main altar accompanied on either side by representations of San Francisco and San Antonio de Padua, not a statue of the Immaculata.

1834 Inventory of Mission San Diego's Church

(Main altar)	1 Statue of Señor San Diego, 50 ps.
	1 Item of San Francisco, 50 ps.
	1 Item of San Antonio, 50 ps.
	1 Small item of the Virgin of the Pillar, 20 ps. **67**
	1 Small wooden crucifix, 8 ps. **68**
(Side altar)	1 Large crucifix, 80 ps.
	1 Framed painting 3 varas (8'3") high of the Last Judgment, 30 ps.
	1 Statue of the Virgin as the Dolores, 80 ps.
(Side altar)	1 Statue of San José, 80 ps.
	1 Purísima and 1 San José, 12 ps. each. **69**
(Nave and baptistry)	2 Framed paintings of the passion, 25 ps. each.
	1 San Diego, 25 ps. **70**
	14 Prints of the passion, 2 ps. each. **71**
	3 Ordinary wooden confessionals, 8 ps.
	1 Virgin as Our Lady of Light, 5 ps. **72**
	1 San Francisco and San Antonio, 25 ps. each. **73**
	1 Framed painting of San Juan Bautista, 5 ps. **74**
	1 Copper baptismal font, 20 ps.

At San Diego Mission, as may be seen from the account of its art holdings, there was no statue of the Immaculate Conception in the mission period, only a small painting of the Virgin of the same denomination, stated to have been as much in the 1779 report when *"tres liensos"* arrived, *"una de la Purísima Concepción, otro de Sn. Joseph de una vara* [2 feet, 9 inches] *y otro de San Juan Bautista bautizando a Jesus Christo de vara y quarta* [3 feet, 5.5 inches] *todo con su media Caña dorado."* **75**

At the Mission up the Valley in 1834, then, there were five statues of commanding size, probably over four feet, one of the patron San Diego, another of San Francisco doubtlessly shown with his Crucifix, a third of San Antonio traditionally represented with an Infant in his arms, a Dolores, and finally a San José, who like San Antonio traditionally held an Infant Child. In addition, there was the near life-size Christ on the Cross. The Nuestra Señora del Pilár was specifically said to be *"chica."* These then were the specific images added to by the effects of the Presidio Church — which should have included the patrona of the City of San Diego in the form of an Immaculata — and whatever other statues originally in that same Church that may reasonably be supposed to have been transferred to the Estudillo House in 1848 and from there to the little Adobe Chapel of the Immaculate Conception ten years later in November of 1858. The probability of their placement there makes necessary a serious appraisal of the photos taken of the interior of this small Chapel in Old Town San Diego before or near the turn of the century.

PHOTOGRAPHIC HISTORY OF MISSION AND PRESIDIO ART OF SAN DIEGO

If it were not for the record kept by local and visiting photographers principally in the Chapel and later in the Church of the Immaculate Conception in Old Town, San Diego, from the 1880's well into the 20th Century, the art of the Mission and Presidio, now widely scattered, would have been lost beyond recall. In the following archival and museum photographs of the greatest importance we are allowed the privilege of examining this art in the past before it left San Diego, thus establishing at least the possibility of its rediscovery in the present.

Photo 1

Interior of the Chapel of the Immaculate Conception in 1889.
The Patroness of San Diego City is to the left on the main altar
and originally from the Presidio.
The large Crucifix and the eight-by-ten-foot painting of the
Last Judgment in the center, are from the Mission.
The San Juan Bautista to the right is from the Presidio.

*An enlargement of the Photo in the Greene collection, and
presumably taken by Pierce, shows the large gold nugget
in the left hand (viewer's right) which eventually would lead to
identification of the statue of the Crucifix in an Indian Village in Arizona.*

Photo 2   LOS ANGELES COUNTY MUSEUM OF NATURAL HISTORY

Photo 6   WHALEY HOUSE, OLD TOWN, SAN DIEGO

*Interior of the Chapel of the
Immaculate Conception circa 1900.
The painting of San Diego de Alcalá
from the Mission is hanging on the wall
of the nave above the sacristy door
on the left or gospel side.*

*Interior of the Chapel of the
Immaculate Conception in 1884.
Detail of Photo 5 showing statue of the
Patron of San Diego Mission with a
vertical crack in the face piece of the head
but with two glass eyes still in
their sockets.*

Photo 3   LOS ANGELES COUNTY MUSEUM OF NATURAL HISTORY

Interior of the Chapel of the Immaculate Conception circa 1900.
The painting of La Madress de la Luz, or Lady of Light,
from the Mission, is hanging on the wall of the nave opposite
the painting of San Diego de Alcalá and above the open doorway
leading into the side chapel on the right or espistle side.

Photo 4

Interior of the Chapel of the Immaculate Conception in 1890's.
View looking through doorway of the side chapel to the right,
showing the statue of the Dolores from the Mission and a large painting
of the Guadalupe and a statue of San Gabriel from the Presidio.

Photo 5   WHALEY HOUSE, OLD TOWN, SAN DIEGO

Interior of the Chapel of the Immaculate Conception in 1884.
View taken from within side chapel on right, showing from left to right:
San Diego de Alcalá, San Gabriel, Ecce Homo, Dolores,
Angel on a Cloud, San Juan Bautista, San Rafael, and
San Miguel amid wax, shell and paper flowers.

Photo 7   WHALEY HOUSE, OLD TOWN, SAN DIEGO

Exterior of the Chapel of the Immaculate Conception perhaps in 1893.
Men and women arranged outside of chapel as art was distributed inside,
as in the missions, separated and appropriately placed with
regard to each sex.

Photo 8   WHALEY HOUSE, OLD TOWN, SAN DIEGO

*Interior of the Chapel of the
Immaculate Conception circa 1893.
Main altar on December 8,
honoring the statue of the
Immaculata.
Note that the large painting
of the Last Judgment,
more appropriately shown with a
work of art like the Crucifix, is
therefore completely covered.*

*Interior of the Chapel of the
Immaculate Conception circa 1900.
View taken from inside sacristy
(room behind the door under the painting
of San Diego on left in Photo 1)
showing Mission baptismal font, trunks,
and vestments with their chest.*

Photo 9   35

Photo 10   TITLE INSURANCE & TRUST CO., LOS ANGELES

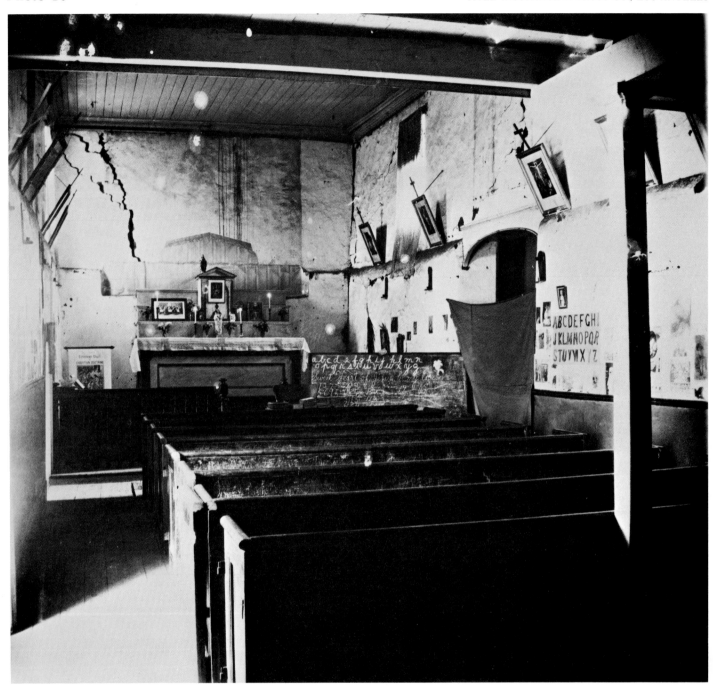

Interior of the Chapel of the Immaculate Conception before 1920.
Mission period art has been removed to the new Church of the
Immaculate Conception on San Diego Avenue, Old Town,
except for the prints of the Stations of the Cross.
The building was still in use as a school.

Photo 11

SANTA BARBARA MISSION ARCHIVES

Interior of the Church of the Immaculate Conception circa 1930.
Museum photograph of mission period art showing statues of
San Diego de Alcalá, the Immaculate Conception, the Cristo Grande,
San Gabriel, the Dolores, the Angel on a Cloud,
San Juan Bautista in the vestibule.

Photo 12

Interior of the Church of the Immaculate Conception circa 1930.
Painting of the Last Judgment from the Mission is in the vestibule
to the left of the altar and statues.

Photo 13

LAMADRESS DLALV

Interior of the Church of the Immaculate Conception circa 1930.
Painting of La Madress de la Luz before restoration,
in the vestibule to the right of the altar and statues.

Photos of Long Ago Turn Up Lost Art in Old Town Chapel

With the Presidio and Mission Churches either in ruin or abandoned to other uses, the art of the mission period was literally piled into the Adobe Chapel of the Immaculate Conception in Old Town San Diego. There professional and amateur photographers alike with cameras of all sizes including the large and cumbersome eight-by-ten-inch size were drawn like moths to a spitting light. The result was a complete record of the art within this small Chapel on Conde Street in Old Town.

More often than not the photo survives today unidentified, but occasionally the last name of its creator is found on the photo, like Slocum from San Diego or Pierce from Los Angeles, but sometimes even this is misleading. Photographers in this time period often copied each other's work, so that a Pierce photo may actually have been taken by James and a Greene almost certainly by Putnam. The study is yet to be made which will identify all of these individuals and clarify these complex interrelationships.

Important collections significant to San Diego are to be found at the Los Angeles County Museum of Natural History, in the Santa Barbara Mission archives, the files of the Title Insurance and Trust Company, which subsequently were conveyed to the care of the California Historical Society, and locally, in the Whaley House maintained in Old Town, by the County of San Diego.

What is certain is that these collections of museum-quality photos (approximately 25,000 negatives in the Greene collection alone) possess a relevance to this history. In the small but important selection to follow, they do nothing less than allow us to enter the small Adobe Chapel on Conde Street at or near the turn of the century and examine almost anything we choose in detail.

Photo 1 — Interior of the Chapel of the Immaculate Conception in 1889.

The first object to strike the eye in this excellent view of the interior of the Adobe Chapel of the Immaculate Conception shown in Photo 1 from the Title Insurance and Trust Company of Los Angeles is the beautiful, nearly life-size statue of the Immaculate Conception, standing on the main altar to the left of the large central Crucifix balanced on the right by the statue of San Juan Bautista. Even from this distance the face appears "sweet, simple, mild, and on the head rests the high, branching golden crown" as Lillian Whaley would describe it four years later in 1893. Surely this is the long lost patrona of San Diego City itself, in whose honor this very Church was named, for whom the City *aniversario* balls were given every December 8, and to whom equal dignity was afforded in the Presidio Church on the hill as stated by Lieutenant Zúñiga in 1790.

The Crucifix in the center can be no other than the one referred to in the 1834 inventory of Mission San Diego where it was listed with just such an enormous painting of the Last Judgment as may be seen behind and above the altar in this photo, the same Crucifix, doubtlessly, placed on the table in the ceremonies designed to lay the Church cornerstone in 1851 "towards which [cross] the procession [from the Estudillo House] wended its way with solemn chants," and undoubtedly the same object damaged subsequently, just a few days before the dedication of this Adobe Chapel in 1858, when "a citizen of the town ... [was found] mounted on the top of the altar, embracing a figure of Christ on the Cross, which is very large, franticly *(sic)* imploring him to hear, and in his delirium he had broken off the arms and otherwise disfigured the body." **76** Under extreme magnification in other photos, these cracks may be detected especially where the left arm (to the viewer's right) meets the shoulder.

The statue of San Juan Bautista (St. John the Baptist) to the right never was at the Mission up the Valley and so must have come with the Immaculata on the other side of the altar from the Presidio Church where a large baptistry side chapel has only recently been excavated. **77** The most striking anomaly in this photo, however, is the fact that the patrona of the Church is placed to the side instead of in the center directly above the tabernacle. With only one altar, artistic balance alone, however, would not allow it. Still this Virgin's crescent moon may be seen in that central position, directly underneath the base of the large *Cristo Grande*. At different times of the year this central Cross would be removed, as may be seen in other photos, the large painting of the *Día del Juicio Universal* covered over, and the patroness placed in the center upon her crescent moon.

The four Stations of the Cross visible on the side walls in Photo 1 are prints and are doubtlessly the same as those listed in the 1834 inventory of the Mission that may be traced back to the period before the 1775 uprising. The most interesting paintings from the standpoint of demonstrating the connection between these art objects and those formerly at the Mission Church are the ones in the upper left-hand corner of Photo 1 and directly opposite in the corresponding upper right-hand corner. Upon careful examination, these paintings disclose the lower portion of a standing figure in Franciscan habit wearing sandals, on the left and the bottom quarter of a depiction of the Virgin as Our Lady of Light, on the right.

Photo 2 — Interior of the Chapel of the Immaculate Conception. Painting of San Diego de Alcala.

In Photo 2 from the Greene collection at the Los Angeles County Museum of Natural History this painting to the left is shown much more clearly. The art objects of Mission San Diego have been missing for so long that most specialists in the field of California mission history would have difficulty recognizing a representation of this patron even if it appeared right before their eyes. Here this lay brother in his Franciscan habit with his log-cross and flowering loaf of bread has his name "San Diego de Alcalà" placed plainly in large gold capitals on the left-hand portion of this dark canvas, making the identification certain. Without this saint's readily detachable symbols in his hands, San Diego in statue form especially, is easily confused with other Franciscan saints, San Antonio or even San Francisco.

Directly across from this depiction of San Diego in Photo 1, hanging on the right wall above the doorway leading into the side chapel on the epistle side, may be detected the lower portions of the other painting. This may be seen in full in Photo 3, also from the Greene collection in Los Angeles.

Photo 3 — La Madress de la Luz.

Here is one of the oldest paintings in the San

Diego collection, said to have been very old in 1783 when it was first inventoried at the Mission as a Nuestra Señora de la Luz, a title which implies both Our Lady of Light and Birth. The angel on the right is seen holding up a basket of hearts, symbols of the life-giving force of the soul, while the Virgin herself holds in her right hand on one level of interpretation the as yet unborn body which is about to be given this life-giving principle. This was one of the two paintings specifically stated to have escaped the roaring flames in 1775 at Mission San Diego.

If one carefully examines this third photo, he will observe in the darkened doorway an upper portion of a painting of Our Lady of Guadalupe and to the left the folded hands of a statue. In Photo 4 by Blunt dated 1903, in the Special Collections at U.C.L.A., this image of the Guadalupe and its accompanying statue may be seen more clearly.

Photo 4 — The Side Chapel Viewed Through the Doorway.

To the left more importantly is seen an excellent Dolores, placed in the 1834 inventory of Mission San Diego with and no doubt under the magnificent passion-size Crucifix which then formed one of the side altars of the Mission. But where is the statue of the patron San Diego?

In Photo 1, a good-sized *santo* may be seen to the far right, just inside this small side chapel. However, no identification can be made from that viewpoint. Photo 5, taken from Lillian Whaley's album, assembled apparently on February 28, 1906 and presently in the Whaley House in Old Town, San Diego, was taken from within this side chapel.

Photo 5 — Side Chapel with Statues.
Photo 6 — Side Chapel: Detail — Statue of San Diego de Alcala.

In photo 5 the Dolores is seen again, San Juan Bautista in front below just to the right, three medium-sized angels scattered about, a smaller one in the foreground directly beneath the Virgin, and an equally small *Ecce Homo* in a seated position to its left. Even farther to the left in this same photo may be seen far more clearly the statue that is almost certainly the

lost patron of San Diego Mission, as in Photo 6. He stands full length, attired in a Franciscan habit; however, he does not possess any identifying emblems. His arms are seen jesticulating outward, perhaps in a welcoming gesture, too high and too far apart to hold the traditional Infant of San Antonio de Padua, while his beardless state precludes a San Francisco identification. If the figure is examined under extreme magnification a small reliquary hole may be detected in his chest, possibly characteristic of San Diego images. **78**

Even though the mission statues of San Francisco, San Antonio, and San José were never photographed in this small Chapel in Old Town San Diego, there can be little doubt that those images shown there at the turn of the century constituted the greater portion of the lost art treasures of the Mission of San Diego. Moreover, not only the presence of the Immaculata but that of all of the other images not listed in the 1834 inventory but shown in the Adobe Chapel suggest very strongly that the Presidio Chapel images were brought there as well. This is an invaluable find.

Prior to this we have known little to nothing about the statues and paintings once in the Chapel of the Port of San Diego. In the 1783 inventory of the Mission we are told that the non-square, oblong painting about two varas high, or five feet six inches, of San Diego de Alcalá was placed in the Presidio Church. But even this meager information was taken from us, for at the end of the Bancroft copy of this Mission's annual reports from 1777 to 1784 is appended a note stating that this painting was returned to the Mission in 1790 by Lieutenant Zúñiga, the same year that this *comandante* recorded the receipt of the statue of the *Inmaculada*.

With this new information, we may feel relatively certain that the three medium-sized angels, the two smaller figures and the Bautista — along with this Immaculata of course — came from the Presidio Church.

How these images were deployed at the Mission and Presidio shall be dealt with more fully later; however, their use here in the Adobe Chapel in Old Town represented that earlier practice in microcosm.

In all surviving photos of the interior of this

small Chapel the images are shown to be placed to the left and right — as was mission practice — appropriate to each sex, male or female, who were separated to the left and right both here in this little Chapel and throughout the mission churches generally. Always is seen the painting of San Diego de Alcalá holding his large Cross to the left while opposite him on the wall to the right hung the depiction of Nuestra Señora de la Luz (Our Lady of both Light and Birth) shown with the Infant in her arms. In fact as late as the early 1900's, as shown in Photo 4, all of the principal images inside the small side Chapel to the right were feminine; the delicate statue of the Dolorosa and the even larger painting of the Guadalupe were seen there. This placement corresponded, moreover, to the way men and women assembled not only here in this little Adobe Chapel but throughout the California missions as well, which gave this art an added behavioral significance.

Perhaps the earliest depiction of a group of individuals standing before a church in California may be found in the sketch of Mission San Carlos, by the French explorer, Jean Francois de la Pérouse. This sketch later was copied by a member of the Spanish exploring and scientific expedition under Captain Alejandro Malaspina. There the mission Indians are lined up to the left and right with respect to their sex, the men on one side and the women, still bare-breasted after sixteen years of mission life, on the other. Perhaps the last Spanish-American grouping of this kind recorded in photograph in the last century may be found in Lillian Whaley's album of views of Old Town San Diego, where the congregation is shown lined up outside of the Adobe Chapel of the Immaculate Conception (covered at this time with wooden siding) as that group would have seated itself in the Church, with the men to the left (inside the Church under the painting of San Diego holding his large Cross), and the women to the right (inside under the depiction of Our Lady of Light and adjacent to the side chapel of the two Virgins).

Photo 7 — The Men to Left, Women to Right.

This careful placement of images with respect to the way men and women assembled themselves in churches in California was not the peculiarity of the Spanish nor the Franciscans in this relatively small portion of the globe. It constitutes, this author feels, one of the principal mechanisms of the development of Western man in his formative or medieval state. For in such an arrangement, these images although certainly viewed devotionally as religious objects, would at the same time by virtue of their placement serve as models or archetypes to the men and women similarly separated in the church and thereby take on the hitherto unsuspected non-religious behavioral functions of the greatest importance to the community.

And yet it takes a certain imagination to see this medieval universe in a grain of sand mirrored in this simple Adobe Chapel at Old Town. One of the major problems was the number of altars in the main body of the Chapel, only one. Under this restriction, the various statues had to be moved about depending upon the feast day or time of year. On Good Friday and Easter, the Dolores would be taken out of her hiding place in the little side chapel to the right and brought into the Church proper, decorated appropriately:

A heavy black curtain was suspended across the chancel, the whole width of the church, completely hiding the altar. Three large white crosses, the central one the largest, adorned the curtain. In the centre of the chancel at the foot of the curtain stood the Madonna [i.e., the Dolores], draped in solemn black. Her clasped hands and uplifted eyes seemed to plead piteously and imploringly for her beloved Son who lay stretched in agony upon the cross at her feet ... Three of the older women in black dresses with black shawls over their heads represented the three Marys. All was gloom. From Good Friday evening until Easter Morning [on Sunday] the church was never alone, night or day. One or the other or all of the three Marys were in constant and devout attendance. Their meals were brought to them. Occasionally one of the three would begin a mournful chant singing in a loud, monotonous voice for some time, the sad notes of some wild *Miserere* ...

[However], on Easter Morning the entire population [would appear no doubt as shown above] in gala attire ... The solemn, black curtain is dropped and the altar, gorgeously decorated, bursts upon the sight. It is a bewildering, dazzling mixture of saints and flowers, tall candlesticks, lighted candles and tapers. The Madonna, no longer in trailing mourning, but beautifully robed occupies an exalted position on the altar. The clasped hands and uplifted face now seem to bespeak joy, ecstacy, infinite gratitude. **79**

On December 8 in 1893 the statue of the Immaculate Conception occupied this central position of honor as may be seen in another view of this little Chapel's interior, taken from Miss Whaley's album of photos.

Photo 8 — Main Altar of Adobe Chapel, December 8.

There may be seen the "bank of flowers," the "tall candlesticks holding lighted candles ... arranged regularly amidst flowers," the "snowy linen cloth with an edging of heavy Spanish lace ... with the long ends folded over toward the front and pinned," and even (under magnification) the "bouquet of flowers" in the hands of the central Immaculata.

In this Chapel in the description and photograph a second principle of iconographic placement may be inferred that all the paintings and statues in the Church had been conceived to relate to two possible emotional conditions clearly and dramatically described in Lillian Whaley's account of the interior of the Old Adobe Chapel from Good Friday, when only the images exposed related to death and the Crucifixion, to Easter, when the flowers, clothing, decorations of all kinds burst forth through the gloom of the previous days' vigils of mourning into a joyous affirmation of life.

All images throughout the missions of California fell into either one of these two categories, and as the former, they might reasonably be classed cross-santos or santas because they were more commonly than not actually depicted with or holding a Cross, just as the latter might just as reasonably be deemed birth-images because they were more often than not actually shown, whether male or female, statue or painting, holding the Infant Child in their hands and appropriately decorated, just as the Easter morning altar described above, with flowers.

No better example of such a division could be found than in the two principal paintings hanging on either side of this Church interior. "Over the inner door of the north wing," Miss Whaley relates, "hangs a full-length portrait of Saint Diego, the patron saint of the place," which she elsewhere describes as holding a large pole Cross (i.e., appropriately classed a cross-santo). "On the opposite door hangs a painting called Our Lady of Light," (or of Birth) and already shown holding an Infant Child in her hands. These respective santos, San Diego and Nuestra Señora de la Luz, and more importantly the emotional and psychological states of mind attendant upon them — seriousness on the one hand and jubilance or joy on the other — were associated both in dress and manner with the men and women who stood themselves separated in the Church underneath these same images. As did these men and women in the Church, so too were these different types of images kept physically separate one from the other. For instance, when the beautiful statue of the Immaculata — here and throughout the missions traditionally a birth-santa — was shown on the main altar amidst a "bank of flowers" on December 8, Miss Whaley was careful to note as can actually be seen in Photo 8 that "long lace curtains completely hid the old painting which hangs back of the altar, a rude representation of the Day of Judgment." This sobering Judgment scene which contains in its middle a representation of the Cross would have been conceived incompatible with the statue of the Immaculata whose tunic was festooned with flowers when the latter was placed in the center or titular position of the altar. Therefore, the large, contradictory image of the Judgment was simply covered over.

In the missions of California, these same principles applied. There, however, the separation of such sad and joyous works of art was accomplished more permanently, more systematically, and more apparently because each type was generally relegated to a separate and relatively permanent altar arrangement. For these mission churches possessed from two to four more side altars than the Adobe Chapel of the Immaculate Conception in Old Town San Diego. However, Miss Whaley recorded other facts of less general significance concerning Mission and Presidio Church properties at the Adobe Chapel during her visit there in 1893.

"The tin candlesticks still occupy their old places on the adobe wall below and between the holy pictures of the estaciones which rest on a projection in the wall," she continued to write; and furthermore noted that "in the north wing is the great chest of drawers which held the costly gold trimmed silken robes in white and scarlet and purple and yellow brocades worn by the priests, the white-linen altar cloths, etc., trimmed in heavy Spanish lace; the great stands of wax and paper and shell flowers in all colors,"[80] as may be seen in part in a photo of this sacristy taken from an exquisite eight-by-ten-inch glass plate negative, now in the Greene collection at the Los Angeles County Museum of Natural History.

Photo 9 — Adobe Chapel Sacristy.

These vestments, statues, and paintings, baptismal font, etc., did not possess an historic value alone. They were virtual treasures of mission art in themselves. The large eight-foot canvas of the Last Judgment placed behind the main altar of this small Adobe Chapel directly in back of the Crucifix of near life size was not as Miss Whaley had characterized it "a rude representation of the Day of Judgment," but by far the best of its kind certainly in all of the missions of California. It is a magnificent composition whose history alone will demand a separate article at the very least. The Immaculata surely is one of the finest statues of the Virgin in the mission system. And the *Cristo Grande* must be examined carefully, for it is the work of a master. Still, despite their value and in spite of the caution taken by individuals like Miss Lillian Whaley who took the greatest trouble to describe and even to photograph these images, not a single one of these works of art now remains in San Diego. All have disappeared once again — sometime after the close of the Adobe Chapel as a house of worship in 1915 and certainly after its reopening as a school in 1918. [81]

Photo 10 — Adobe Chapel as School.

This photo of the interior of the Adobe Chapel was taken "after the vestments, paintings, statues, and bells" were removed "from the sixty-seven-year-old adobe chapel,"[82] in 1915 and obviously after Miss Caroline Shannon "reopened the Old Adobe Chapel in 1918 for catechism classes."[83] Seven years after the opening of this little school the Adobe Chapel was condemned by the City for the same reason the art treasures were removed from it. As may be seen especially along the sanctuary wall, the building was literally falling apart, even though it still possessed its main altar, tabernacle, and 18th Century prints of the Stations of the Cross. Miss Whaley recorded this stage of the Chapel in her memoirs: "A visit to the interior will show the original but no longer dependable adobe walls which are seamed and cracked. The pictures of the Stations are still in place on the ledge which juts out from the inner walls and the old tin candlesticks are still in their old places. The Chapel was used till very recently as a kindergarten and school for teaching of the church catechism . . . All church paintings have been removed to the new church."

Shortly afterward in her memoirs, Miss Whaley included everything of value in this statement: "All vestments, saints, holy vessels and paintings . . . have been removed to the new church."[84] In short, whatever was once in the Old Adobe Chapel in the way of art treasures had long since disappeared, leaving the reconstructed and moved Adobe Chapel today without a vestige of these works of art which once graced its now barren walls.

In the 1920's these invaluable objects had been carefully placed in the vestibule of the new Church of the Immaculate Conception in Old Town as was recorded in two photos — the smaller, a snapshot dated 1920 given to this author in 1963 by James W. Doyle, [85] and the larger one, Photo 11, from the photographic collection of Mission Santa Barbara.

Photo 11 — Objects in Vestibule of the Church of Immaculate Conception in the 1930's.

However, not to be outdone, Lillian Whaley at the age of sixty-six took the trouble to go down to this new Church on San Diego Avenue in Old Town with pencil and paper in hand to record the following notes within that vestibule:

Notice in the church, 1930: "These Statues and

Paintings and the Bells in the lower tower are from San Diego Mission."

Title of Picture — Sn. Diego de Alcalá — a Franciscan in brown robe and canted cape and sandals and hanging knotted waist cord, holding with his right hand a rude cross much taller than himself — head bare — the left hand is holding in the upturned corner of his cape what appears to be small loaves of bread strewn with roses.

Sn. Gabriel.

Sn. Juan Bautista.

Crescent underneath the feet of the Virgin. Also cherubs. Entitled — Narracion del Juicio Universal, Confirmada segun testimonio de la Sagrada Escritura (sic) — followed by verses from the Scriptures in Spanish — artist's name not given.

The huge painting entitled *Narracion del Juicio Universal*, as it was seen in the Adobe Chapel, usually had a *Crucifix Grande* in front of it or some other statue blocking this caption described by Lillian Whaley, but here as it hung in the vestibule of the Church of the Immaculate Conception the entire painting could be seen at close range and appreciated in detail despite its imposing size. And, of course, in this position, it attracted the eye of a wandering photographer, very possibly C. C. Pierce.

Photo 12 — Last Judgment, Taken in the 1930's.

Miss Whaley turned from this huge painting on the left wall of the vestibule as she faced the statues, which have been described, on the temporary altar in front of the stained glass window, and turned full around to the opposite wall where she began to copy the following:

Title of Painting — Lamadress de la Luz — painted by Luis S. Menafeci (sic) — Represents the Virgin with the Child on left arm standing on low pedestal surrounded by heads of angels. Right hand supports a brown child — Indian, perhaps — an angel kneels at her right presenting a filled basket. A branched crown above her head is held on each side by two angels (or cherubs). A representation head and face of God and the Holy Spirit represented by a white dove at top of painting. Kneeling figures of man and child in each upper corner. Figures of kneeling Indians, quiver full of arrows on the back of one in the two lower corners. The colors much subdued by time though still beautiful.

This painting, perhaps the oldest then in San Diego, attracted the same photographer's eye.

It is by Luis Mena, whose work shows up also at San Gabriel Mission in the *Gloria* and elsewhere in other missions.

Photo 13 — Nuestra Senora de la Luz, Taken in 1930's.

Finally, Lillian Whaley turned to one more painting:

"Sn. Diego de Alcalá" in prevailing brown. **86**

It would seem almost inconceivable that these art treasures in San Diego's new Church of the Immaculate Conception, despite the sign which announced boldly their historic value to the San Diego community, would nevertheless vanish once again, not only from this vestibule but more importantly from the entire City and even from the memory of all but the most informed. Still without records memory fades. Henry J. Downie, who spent his life tracking down such Mission treasures, and to whom this author is in such great debt, knew of these images in the vestibule of the Church of the Immaculate Conception as a boy and later knew of their dispersal. He had assumed, however, that they had long since been scattered about beyond reclaim. In 1963 James W. Doyle, one of the more knowledgeable men in Old Town San Diego concerning these matters, regrettably admitted too that he had no idea of their whereabouts at that time.

Fourteen years later, after this author had located almost all of these images elsewhere, Doyle's nephew, Charles Hughes of the Serra Museum, provided the missing link somehow overlooked, that would logically explain the removal of these images from San Diego: the Franciscans in the 1920's had taken over the Church of the Immaculate Conception in Old Town in whose vestibule this art was stored. When they left, since the art was obviously not being used and could not be brought to San Diego Mission (then either in ruin or under restoration, etc.), the Franciscans logically brought these images with them to other missions still in their charge, principally to the nearest, Mission San Luis Rey, where they have been well taken care of but to some degree lost to the eye of history.

The missing statue of the patron of San Diego Mission stands today in San Luis Rey Mission Church in one of the niches of the transept side altar to the left, decorated as a San Antonio de Padua. The magnificent patroness of the Presidio and Port of San Diego stands in a museum room of that same Mission relatively neglected when one considers the traditions so richly associated with her throughout the entire development of the City of San Diego to the south especially in the 19th Century. The eight-, in fact, eight-by-ten-foot painting of the Last Judgment, perhaps the finest of its kind in the entire mission system, hangs in a small private chapel just off the sanctuary of the epistle side not generally open to the public, apparently incorrectly believed by some to have been brought to that Mission by the Zacatecan fathers in the 1890's. **87** The Pilár, after whom the mission district of San Diego was named, is at San Juan Capistrano; the San José, which once formed the side altar of San Diego Mission to the right, is at San Antonio de Padua Mission. The statue of San Francisco, mate to the statue of the San Diego, is in the Friars' Chapel of Mission San Miguel. The beautiful *Cristo Grande* of such historic significance to San Diego, now decorates an altar in a small chapel in Guadalupe, Arizona. The Dolores, seen so pathetically every Good Friday with this crucified figure of her Son at her feet and so joyous on Easter for so many years in Old Town, the ancient painting so strangely named "La Madress de la Luz" and so carefully described by Miss Whaley in 1930 in the vestibule of the Church of the Immaculate Conception, the San Juan Bautista, the sacristy chest of drawers, even San Diego's original baptismal font, lie about San Luis Rey Mission, valued indeed and cared for responsibly as much as a mission budget will allow. But the light of history at that Mission today has gone out with regard to the true origins of these works of art.

Yet the physical rediscovery of these invaluable works of art hardly constitutes a final goal. Now that they have been found, they may be measured and compared to the original 1834 inventory. By following this procedure, an investigator is led to the inevitable conclusion that these art objects are in fact the lost art treasures of San Diego Mission, and by so doing he may change a very strong local tradition into incontestable fact.

With the 1834 inventory at hand for comparison, this local tradition which implied that all of these objects of art came from the Mission itself will necessarily have to be modified. For by reference to this document it is learned which images did and which did not come from that Mission. In this way, not only the iconographic system of the Mission but also that of the Presidio Church may be reconstructed, with the latter actually making it possible to appreciate more fully the only lengthy description of any activities in the Church of the Port of San Diego in mission times, the splendid account of the performance of the *Pastores* seen there in 1829 by Alfred Robinson under the direction of Don José Antonio Estudillo. But now that they have been found, these works of art should be exhibited themselves, even the very least piece of which is replete with sufficient historical importance to command genuine interest.

PAINTINGS AND SCULPTURE OF MISSION AND PRESIDIO AS EXISTING TODAY

Scattered throughout four other missions of California in addition to a small Indian village in Arizona, the art once in the Mission and Presidio Churches of San Diego constituted perhaps the largest and most beautifully executed collection of art for a Spanish-American community in the entire United States. That is why so many photographers of the past took such an interest in these subjects, leaving an almost complete archival record of their presence in San Diego. Yet their beauty, charm, and sophistication can not be appreciated unless viewed directly or seen in color as in the following pages.

Photo 15

*California's First Baptismal Font from Mission San Diego, brought to
San Diego by Fray Junípero Serra in 1769 from Baja California.
Now in the sacristy of Mission San Luis Rey.*

Photo 15A

*Vestment Chest from Mission San Diego.
This chest, now in the museum of Mission San Luis Rey, has a small
inlaid fish cut into the wood on either side of each drawer handle.*

Photo 16

Delicately sculptured Angel on a Cloud.
Originally from San Diego's Presidio Church.
Now in the museum of Mission San Luis Rey.

Photo 17

San Gabriel.
One of a group of three archangels,
traditionally placed to the left of center,
from San Diego's Presidio Church.
Now in the museum of
Mission San Luis Rey.

Photo 18

San Miguel.
One of a group of three archangels,
traditionally placed in the center,
from San Diego's Presidio Church.
Now in the church of
Mission San Luis Rey,
high above the main altar to the left.

Photo 19

San Rafael.
One of a group of three archangels,
traditionally placed to the right of center,
from San Diego's Presidio Church.
Now in the church of
Mission San Luis Rey,
high above the main altar to the right.

Photo 20

La Inmaculada Concepción, Patroness of the City of San Diego.
It originally occupied the main altar of San Diego's Presidio Church
since 1790 (probably below the set of three archangels).
Now in the vestment room of Mission San Luis Rey.

Photo 21

Photo 22

*La Inmaculada Concepción,
Patroness of the City of San Diego.
Detail, front.
Already in the 1950's, this naturally graceful
"patrona de los militares en San Diego"
was reported to be, as it still appears today,
termite-ridden.
Now as then it cries out for
competent restoration.*

*San Juan Bautista.
Originally the principal icon of the
recently excavated baptistry on the right
or epistle side of San Diego's
Presidio Church.
Now in the similar chapel at San Luis Rey,
where, as at San Diego Mission, only a
painting of this popular santo
was originally used.*

Photo 24

Photo 25

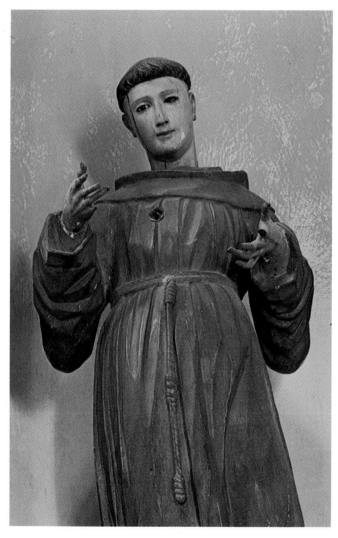

San Diego de Alcalá.
This exceptional piece of hand-carved
statuary is almost certainly the lost patron
of California's first mission at San Diego.
Now above the side altar on the left or
gospel side of Mission San Luis Rey.

San Diego de Alcalá.
Detail, without modern Infant.
Small reliquary hole in statue's breast
may identify it as San Diego de Alcalá.

*Museum Photo of Nuestra
Señora del Pilár at
Mission San Diego before
1905. First published by
George Wharton James in
1905, this photograph of
Our Lady of the Pillar,
as recorded on its back, was
taken at Mission San Diego.
This origin is confirmed
by James, the 1834 inventory
of that Mission, and
San Diego's mission site,
which was named in
honor of this Virgin.*

*Museum Photo of Nuestra Señora del Pilár at
Mission San Juan Capistrano after 1905.
Statues shown in Photos 26 and 27 are the same figure.
Note missing index finger of the Virgin's left hand and
the missing left foot of the Infant in both.*

Photo 28

Photo 23

Nuestra Señora del Pilár.
Originally from Mission San Diego where
it stood above the main altar below the
central statue of the patron.
Now in Serra Chapel,
Mission San Juan Capistrano, this statue,
perhaps the second oldest in California,
has recently been coated with house paint.
It may be identified with the figures in
Photos 26 and 27 by reference to the
worm holes.

Ecce Homo.
Originally from the Presidio,
probably in the mortuary side chapel,
this small, sad figure of Christ under
condemnation is the only work of art
shown in these pages still in San Diego.
It is now at Mission San Diego.

58

Photo 29

Photo 30

San José.
Said to have come originally from
Mission San Diego by the authority
responsible for placing it in its present
location, Mission San Antonio de Padua
near King City, California.
Shown to the right in the oldest photo
of the interior of Mission Santa Barbara
Church, by Vischer, this statue may
have been inventoried at that Mission
in 1858 but not before.

Dolores.
Originally from Mission San Diego where
it occupied the side altar to the left,
below the near life-size depiction of the
Crucifixion, where it was inventoried
in 1834.
Now in the mortuary side chapel on the
right or epistle side of the present church
of Mission San Luis Rey.

Photo 32

The Last Judgment.
Eight-by-ten-foot painting from
San Diego Mission originally placed
above side altar to the left above the
large Crucifix and Dolores.
Now located in the semi-private side chapel
off the sanctuary of Mission San Luis Rey.

Photo 33

Confirmada se

Ifai.C.13.Ves aqui el dia del Señor,q
Malach.Cap.4.Cata aqui el dia que bendra.ense
impiedad,y los quemará como
Joel Cap.3.Levantense,y suban todas las Cientes al Val
Daniel Cap.12.Muchos de aquellos, q̃. duermen en el
Cap.16.El Señor todo poderoso vengará las injuri

Last Judgment, detail: The Damned.
Among the hundreds of human figures ranging in shape from the
grotesque to the beatic, these in the foreground indicate most clearly
the degree to which this artist has mastered color to delineate form.

Photo 34

Last Judgment, detail: The Blessed.
The pastel quality of this portion of San Diego's huge canvas is
symphonically discordant with the darker tones of the condemned
shown above in Photo 33.

Photo 31

The Cristo Grande of Mission San Diego.
Originally occupied the side altar to the left at the Mission,
above the Dolores and below the large Last Judgment.
Detached from its original wooden cross and restored almost beyond
recognition, this magnificent work nevertheless stands in Arizona
with San Diego's rich and colorful history forming a sunset of
recollections behind it.

Photo 35

*The Last Judgment of
Mission Santa Barbara.
Presently at Mission San
Antonio de Padua, this
painting is a relatively poor
copy not of the San Diego
Last Judgment, nor is it a
copy of a similar work in
the Prado or Escorial, in
Spain as alleged, but of the
original from which both
paintings derived and now
located in the
Louvre in France.*

*Nuestra Señora de la Luz.
Restored painting of
Our Lady of Light
from Mission San Diego
now at
Mission San Luis Rey
in the mortuary chapel and
so grossly overpainted and
modernized that its
mission period style is
hardly recognizable.*

Photo 36

Photo 37

San Diego de Alcalá, earliest painting.
Supplied for Mission San Diego before its founding in 1769
but not discovered aboard the packet boat San Antonio
until the following year, 1770, this historic piece is now hanging in
Mission San Luis Rey's Church sacristy.

Photo 38

*Largest painting of San Diego de Alcalá.
Originally at Mission San Diego,
possibly before 1775,
this depiction of the Mission's patron,
shown holding his traditional log-cross
and flowering bread, is now hanging in
Mission San Luis Rey's nave, epistle side.*

Photo 39

*Last painting of San Diego de Alcalá.
Referred to by Lillian Whaley in Old Town,
San Diego, as the patron of
Mission San Diego in "prevailing brown,"
this smaller painting, which replaced the
one shown in Photo 38 in 1783, now hangs
in the museum of Mission San Luis Rey.*

Search Reveals the Present Locations of Mission Era Art

The statues of the patrons in the twenty-one missions of California were generally received according to a pattern; they normally replaced the painting of the favored saint on the celebration of the tenth year of the mission's existence. Founded in 1798, for example, Mission San Luis Rey, just to the north of San Diego, received the statue of its patron which is now at Pala, in 1808. San Diego, both at the Presidio and at the Mission, failed to meet this deadline.

Since no official records have been found as yet for the Presidio, little may be said about the acquisition dates of its rich and prestigious supply of statues except to suggest that the most impressive piece of its entire holdings, the Immaculata, probably arrived in 1789 for the twentieth *aniversario*, although the event was not reported until February of the following year by Lieutenant José Zúñiga, the Presidio's *comandante*.

By contrast, Mission San Diego may boast as complete a set of annual reports as any other mission, yet strangely they do not record any of the arrival dates of the Mission statuary beyond 1777. However, from other documents, we know that the Mission still lacked a statue of its patron in 1783, which was in fact first recorded "on April 26, 1804" in the Mission's burial register when a grave stone marker was placed "next to the statue of San Diego," possibly received either in 1789 or 1799. Still, in 1804, from the same source, we know that the bulk of the statuary, the San José, the San Antonio de Padua, the San Francisco, the *Cristo Grande*, and the Dolores had not arrived yet. The San José was first mentioned in the burial register in August of 1807 and the San Francisco "in his niche" in 1816.

The complete holdings of the Mission were probably in place by the dedication of the present Church on November 12, 1813. All but one statue, the San Antonio, and two small paintings, of the Purísima and a San José, survive. But perhaps of greater surprise is the even higher survival rate of the numerous works of art originally from the Presidio.

Photo 15 — California's First Baptismal Font.

Photo 15A — San Diego Mission's Vestment Chest.

Perhaps the oldest object in the entire collection of art treasures originally from San Diego is the simple baptismal font. After the 1775 Indian revolt at San Diego when the effects of the Mission Church were being retabulated and distinguished from those of the Presidio Chapel, this font was specifically stated to be "destinada al Servicio de la Yglesia" of the Mission, **88** where it was itemized at the close of the mission period in 1834 as the *"bautisterio de cobre."* In 1848, it came to Old Town. Behind it, the Mission, along with the entire missionary enterprise in Alta California, was in ruin, just as had happened previously in Baja California. For before being brought to the San Diego area in 1769, this same font had served either at Mission San Luis Gonzaga or Nuestra Señora de los Dolores in Lower California, for thirty-two or forty-eight years. These two establishments to the south with their remaining Indian families were dissolved in 1769 and their church goods, including this font, appropriated for the new missions to the north. **89** Yet perhaps the font did not speak of such hopes in life. Its cover still possesses the mystical eight-sided pattern traditionally associated with baptismal fonts from the earliest times in the Church when man's life was given a seven-fold division from the cradle to the grave, while here the eighth represented in baptism the promise of life beyond death.**90**

When brought to Upper California in 1769, this *bautisterio* did go to Mission San Diego, not to San Carlos established the next year in Monterey, where even as late as the 1835 inventory no such copper vessel was recorded at this, the second mission founded in the chain of twenty-one. Furthermore, no Spanish document speaks of a similar vessel for the Port and Military Chapel at San Diego, although a baptistry side chapel was eventually built on to the Presidio Church; however, the *pila* itself must have been constructed of stone or masonry as at San Juan Capistrano, an hypothesis supported by the recent discovery of "fragments of a steatite bowl ... in the trash deposit south of the baptistry" **91** appropriate to such a use, and by the fact that only one copper font survived the destruction of the two Churches of San Diego after the mission period.

In the photo of the sacristy of the Adobe Chapel in Old Town shown in Photo 9, this font is seen on the floor to the right of what is very possibly one of the three original China trunks which Serra packed with his own hands in 1769 in La Paz but which now may be found in the vestment room of the museum of San Luis Rey Mission, where the aspergil bucket seen above may be found as well, however in the library room. In Photo 9, on the trunk may be seen a second vessel, bronze and dishlike in shape, commonly referred to as a tray or *bandeja* in Spanish; this was positioned under the head of thousands of Indian neophyte infants at San Diego Mission while a silver conch or shell-like scoop, as yet lost, was used to dip the holy water out of this large copper *bautisterio* which is presently located in the sacristy at Mission San Luis Rey.

At that Mission three important inventories were made in this century which disclosed that important establishment's works of art and mission vestments, in one case with important and informative commentary added by the Reverend Dominic Gallardo, O.F.M., who at mid-century had been associated with San Luis Rey since 1912. The first of these documents was drawn up by the Zacatecan fathers on February 5, 1903, and lists the contents of the Church and sacristy at that time. All images are listed on one page; none of which with one possible exception could possibly refer to the San Diego images later brought to that Mission in later years, and the exception is a correspondence in name alone as the contemporary photographs of that period demonstrate. The second inventory was drawn up by Rino Lanzoni apparently between 1947 and 1954. Since the Lanzoni numbering system was employed by the more important 1954 inventory commented upon by Father Dominic, the same shall be used here.

Lanzoni numbers the San Diego font 148 but incorrectly asserts it to be the "original ... of Pala Mission," an oversight corrected by Father Dominic:

"Correction of No. 148 of Mr. Lanzoni's notes: the baptismal font ... came from San Diego Mission. Not from Pala, as Mr. Lanzoni has it in his notes."

(Size: Diameter 16.5 inches, height, 9.5 inches.)

Even the Mission's vestment chest, which can

be seen in part in Photo 9, has been located at Mission San Luis Rey, in the museum. Its dimensions are, top, seven feet, five inches. It was inventoried at the Mission in 1834 as six feet, ten and a half inches, by two feet, nine inches.

Photo 16 — Angel on Cloud.

Among the statues and paintings photographed in the Adobe Chapel in Old Town, some are known never to have been at the Mission. One of the least of these, shown on the left-hand side of the Chapel in Photo 1, is the angel kneeling on a cloud, nevertheless, not without his peculiar charm when seen here for the first time in full view. Lanzoni number 224, said to be from San Diego Mission by Father Dominic. Size: 24.5 inches. See Photos 1, 5, and 11.)

Photo 17 — San Gabriel.
Photo 18 — San Miguel.
Photo 19 — San Rafael.

As shown also in Photo 1, on either side of the main altar, may be seen the archangels San Miguel on the left and San Gabriel on the right, while in Photo 5 all three may be seen, San Gabriel to the left of the central Dolores, San Rafael just to her right, and San Miguel even further right. (Each of these figures is the same size in Photo 5 although wide-angle lens distortion does not make them appear so.) The value of the discovery of this set of archangels can hardly be overestimated. They allow us to reconstruct almost entirely the sanctuary design of San Diego's Presidio Church, where they were undoubtedly placed high above the main altar over the head of the statue of the Immaculate Conception, thus forming a pattern that may be found throughout all of Mexico, a fact never published before and therefore not commonly known. Three such angels, for instance, may be found above the altarpiece devoted to the Guadalupe at the Church of Sta. Rosa in Querétero, where Michael is seen directly above the Virgin, San Gabriel to his right (viewer's left), and San Rafael to his left. The same is seen in the Church of Valenciana, where San Miguel is shown again above the Guadalupe with Gabriel on the viewer's left again and San Rafael on his right with

the four additional archangels added two and two. (See Figures 1, 2, 3.)

The same may be found in the Borda Church in Tasco, in the Shrine of Ocotlán, and in many others, while the same arrangement is found in other California missions, San Antonio de Padua pre-eminently, where, however, the paintings of the subsidiary angels San Gabriel and San Rafael were reversed in the 1870's because the iconographic polarities of that Mission Church had been reversed. The side altar to the left (devoted to the Passion) had fallen and its effects transferred to the right side altar formerly devoted to the Guadalupe. Such statues were placed in accordance with a pattern as common as the Dolores and San Juan at the foot of the Cross. A knowledge of this pattern allows one, in the complete absence of documentation, to place these angels back in their original position in the Presidio Chapel from which they came with a high degree of reliability even in the absence of any definite knowledge of the interior appearance of that historic Church building. Lanzoni numbers 131, 288, and 289, all three of which are said to have come from Mission San Diego by Father Dominic, in the June 21 - 22, 1954, inventory of San Luis Rey Mission compiled by Father Geoffrey Bridges, O.F.M. These angels in fact, however, came from the Presidio.

(Sizes: 34.5 inches. See Photos 1, 5 and 11.)

Photo 20 — La Inmaculada Concepcion, Patroness of the City of San Diego.

The historical value of this statue of the Immaculate Conception to the development of the City of San Diego is great. She presided over the Presidio Church as the patroness of the Port as early as 1790 at which time the painting of San Diego formerly placed above the main altar of that Church was sent back to the Mission, thereby leaving her in complete command. A statue in this same presentment had been left there twenty years earlier in 1770 by Serra himself when he moved northward to found California's second mission. The crescent moon base (8 inches high and 28.5 inches from tip to tip) beneath the feet of this beautiful image is a little larger than might be expected for a statue this size (without crown and base, 41 inches high) and may be the original support for the first statue of the Immaculata, which was four and a half feet tall, brought up from Baja California in 1769 and stolen by the Indians from Mission San Diego in 1775. In the panic, the Indians would not likely have taken both the statue and its large, awkwardly handled base as they ran off into the night. In the case of the San José also stolen, even the small infant was apparently dropped and, therefore, later found and returned. Yet the historical significance of this gracious statue is secondary to its beauty.

Photo 21 — Detail of Immaculate Conception, Front.

No other statue in all of the twenty-one missions of California, with the possible exception of the *Rosario* at Santa Inés Mission, matches her charm. From the rear she is equally striking, her long auburn hair, beautifully carved, falls on her shoulders amidst a sprinkle of golden stars that decorate her gracefully draped tunic.

A careful inspection of Photos 20 and 21 will demonstrate how desperately this precious statue stands in need of care. Already in the 1940's Lanzoni noted the "termites at work!" The cuff of the left sleeve is completely eaten away from the sleeve, yet the damage is yet minimal but will only remain so if proper care is taken. Expert restoration is needed but at the same time one must give thanks that this beautiful piece has not as yet been touched by the hand of an amateur as was allowed to happen — to everyone's horror — to the priceless statuary at San Juan Capistrano only recently, where, one of the important statues from San Diego was involved. Lanzoni number 114, said to have come from San Diego Mission by Father Dominic, but actually from the Presidio.

(Size: 56.5 inches high. See Photos 1, 8, and 11.)

Photo 22 — Statue of San Juan Bautista.

One of the last important archaeological discoveries made at the Church site on Presidio Hill was the existence of a semicircular side baptistry chapel where, there can be little doubt, the statue of San Juan Bautista, shown in Photo 22 and recently restored, was placed upon a wall bracket much as it may be presently seen in the baptistry at San Luis Rey,[91] where in the mission period, according to that Mission's 1844 inventory, there was merely a modest sized painting of the *"Bautismo de Christo por San Juan,"* (2 feet, 9 inches high by 1 foot, 10 inches wide). The existence of this statue, therefore, confirms the identification of that side chapel foundation at the Presidio Church, the epistle side, as a baptistry, for such a statue hardly could have been given less honor in view of the fact that the Mission itself at San Diego possessed only a painting of the same subject according to its own 1834 inventory. The Lanzoni number was 260; "from San Diego Mission," according to Father Dominic, but actually from the Presidio.

(Size: 44 inches high. See Photos 1, 5, and 11.)

Photo 23 — Ecce Homo.

The small statue of the Ecce Homo shown in Photo 5, and again in Photo 23 as it exists today, is the only piece of the entire mission period collection that is presently in San Diego, and since this work deals with the lost treasures of San Diego, it shall be presented here without comment except to say that it was not originally at the Mission where it may be found today but rather in the Presidio Church of San Diego, probably placed in the "mortuary" side chapel. Furthermore, although the painting of the Guadalupe in the side chapel at Old Town (Photos 3, 4, and 5) is of the same approximate size as the one at San Luis Rey in the large gilded frame (reportedly smuggled out of Mexico by the Zacatecan fathers and brought ashore at Oceanside in the 1890's), the two paintings are absolutely distinct. The one in Old Town hung in all probability, if it did not form a side altar in the Presidio Church, on the epistle side opposite the mortuary chapel.[92] These, then, were the lost art objects in the Presidio Church.

Photo 24 — San Diego de Alcala.

This patron of the Mission San Diego de Alcalá has never before been recognized as such in writing and has been photographed only twice. (See Photos 5, 6, and 11.) Establishing the identity of this santo, therefore, is of the first order of importance. Having been photographed in the Adobe Chapel of Old Town, it may be safely asserted to have come from the Mission up the Valley where it could have been identified in only two possible ways, either as the Mission's patron or as a San Antonio de Padua. The strongest argument in favor of the latter identification is found in the hair. In the three paintings of San Diego de Alcalá (Photos 37 - 39) to survive Mission San Diego's destruction, in one painting that may be seen in Pedro Rojas' *Historia General del Arte Mexicano, Época Colonial*, by Baltazar de Echave Orio, and finally on the only statue of this saint identified by name in California, and presently in the Serra Museum, San Diego is shown without a tonsured hair styling. This point might be considered conclusive if this saint was never shown with the tonsured cut which, however, is not the case as may be seen in the frontispiece of Engelhardt's separate work on San Diego Mission. There the saint is presented exactly as he is shown in this statue. The hair, then, cannot be a deciding factor.

The second point that would at first appear to support a San Antonio identification would be the position of the hands and arms. This led the fathers at San Luis Rey to place a modern infant in the cradle position, and nothing could more clearly demonstrate the incorrectness of this assumption. When San Antonio or any real human cradles an infant, he places one hand under the child, not one at the head and the other at the tip of the toes as is seen in the case of this statue, whose eyes, moreover, pass so completely over the superimposed infant that it cannot be doubted that the child never was intended to be there. When a statue is poorly made, none of these considerations need apply, but in the case above of a santo obviously turned by the hand of a master — look at the rendering of the habit which is not gesso but hand carved or examine the hands — they are decisive.

When the child is taken away, moreover, there is revealed a hole right to the left center of the santo's breast which if functional may have supported the flowering loaves of bread once in the saint's hands, or, if not, then perhaps more convincingly it was a reliquary hole.

Photo 25 — Detail of San Diego Without the Infant.

Historically, this hole is traceable to other depictions of this saint. At first it appears merely as a rent in the fabric of this saint's habit, to suggest his austere and astringent mode of life; then it becomes larger as is seen here, probably acting as a repository for a small relic, and finally it takes on gigantic proportions as seen in the San Diego santo now in the Serra Museum of Old Town, where the hole in the chest nearly approaches the proportions of the figure's head. But these reasons are not conclusive either.

Without looking at the wide-placed hands or this hole in the breast but only at this saint's head, one might reasonably accede to the San Diego identification because that face simply does not reflect in any way the childlike warmth generally given to the countenance of San Antonio de Padua, commonly shown gazing in rapture directly at the tiny Infant Child resting in his arms or on his book. Here more appropriately, an ascetic San Diego is seen, lean of face, possessing greater austerity if not a certain severity. When compared to the other depictions of the same saint from San Diego Mission, this appearance simply must be said to be characteristic of that Mission's patron. The four surviving images, including this statue and the three surviving paintings (Photos 37, 38, and 39), all have that long neck and even longer nose for the proportions of the face. All of these facts, the apparently full head of hair, the wide, apparently jesticulating positioning of the hands and arms, the otherwise unaccountable hole in the breast, certainly carved intentionally, and finally and most convincingly, the actual appearance of this saint's face, lead one to believe with caution that this may indeed be the patron of the first mission to be founded in California. That was why, no doubt, it alone of the three Franciscan santos originally at the Mission at San Diego was left behind, treasured and protected throughout the years when the other two images, San Francisco and San Antonio, were allowed to be taken to other missions at an early date. The Lanzoni number is 145: " 'St. Anthony of Padua' — large carved wood figure — grayish-brown finish — Spanish workmanship of the late XVIIth century." Father Dominic, unfortunately, made no comment on this statue.

(Size: 48 inches high; see Photos 1 and especially 46 to 48.)

Nuestra Senora del Pilar

In the mission period at San Diego the sanctuary wall above the main altar was adorned with the statue of the patron San Diego above, a San Francisco probably to the left or gospel side, and a San Antonio de Padua to the right or epistle side, all placed in wall niches as is stated specifically of the San Francisco in a 1816 inventory. [93] Below the central statue of the patron, according to the 1834 inventory, was placed a statue of the Virgin and Child standing on a pillar perhaps two times its own height, probably positioned just above the small Crucifix on the tabernacle. This small statue was a copy of the one carved, according to legend, by Santiago after this Virgin's strange appearance to him on the banks of the Erbo River in Zaragoza, Spain. Because of her placement there, the sanctuary design at San Diego Mission may have been given a cosmological motif. One sees this tradition perhaps most clearly in the Borda Church in Tasco as it exists today on the side altar devoted to this Virgin located immediately to the right as one enters the Church's main doorway. In this case, the Nuestra Señora, surmounted on her wooden pillar, is surrounded by seven angels who apparently originally held the seven planets (the cosmological device). Here in California above the main altar at San Antonio de Padua, originally the central Virgin, although clearly a Purísima, nevertheless stood on a pillar and was therefore surrounded by the entire scholastic universe (another cosmological device). In Los Angeles' Plaza Church before the turn of the century the Purísima there was occasionally elevated upon an even larger pillar, and when this occurred, for example in 1895, as reported in the December issue of *Land of Sunshine*, an appropriate background sprayed with large stars affixed to a cloth was erected which covered the entire sanctuary wall behind the main altar and this elevated Virgin (another cosmological device). Most importantly, this tradition is still maintained to the present day at the original shrine of the Pilár in Spain where a marbled backdrop is filled with sculptured stars.[94]

Photo 26 — The Pilar When at Mission San Diego.
Photo 27 — The Same, Later at Mission San Juan Capistrano.

The statue of the Pilár shown in Photo 26 was photographed at San Diego as is so stated on this print taken from the Title Insurance and Trust Company of Los Angeles, the C. C. Pierce collection, first published by George Wharton James in 1905. [95] Its diminutive size may be gathered from Photo 27 taken at Mission San Juan Capistrano in the same year as James published his book, 1905, where the statue had been taken since the earlier photo of it was made in San Diego. It may be found today at San Juan Capistrano Mission repainted almost beyond recognition.

Photo 28 — Neustra Senora del Pilar: Today.

The statues in the two black and white Photos (26 and 27) may be recognized as the same object by reference to the missing forefinger of the Virgin's left hand and the missing dove and left hand and foot of the Christ Child. All three may be seen to be the same statue by comparing their worm holes.

This diminutive statue's historic importance to the first mission in California on its second or present site lies in the fact that the location of Mission San Diego today was originally named after this Virgin. [96] This small Pilár was first mentioned in the 1777-1784 inventory, for the first year stored away in a box for protection, and may, therefore, have been at the Mission from the start. It was mentioned again in 1782 when its octagonal pillar, now lost, was built and its gilded silver crown came from Mexico, which is also lost, and finally in inventories two more times, in 1783 and 1834.

(Size: 21 inches.)

Photo 29 — San Jose.

According to the 1834 inventory of San Diego there was a side altar devoted to San José, which apparently existed in the Church prior to the present one dedicated on November 12, 1813, for the *Book of Burials* for August 19, 1807, records the fact that Father Nicolás Lázaro was buried "under [the statue of] San José." **97**

In the 1783 inventory, Lasuén stated that the Church then had only two altars, the main and another devoted to Our Lady of Pillar located on the right or epistle side of the Church. However, the new Church of 1804 had two side altars upon its dedication on April 26, 1804, according to the burial register again, with the Pilár then on the left or gospel side altar. **98** Presumably at the same time this San José occupied the right side altar.

As has been explained, **99** this arrangement was "normal" when a mission patron might be deemed a cross-santo which certainly would have been the case when the painting of San Diego with its large log cross was upon the main altar. Then a Cross would have stood outside of the church as the symbol of the mission's foundation, as it were, opposite this log cross on the main altar within the church (cross opposite cross) just as a birth santa, this Virgin holding the Infant in her arms on the side altar to the left would have been seen opposite a birth santo on the right, on the altar of San José also traditionally depicted with such an Infant (birth opposite birth). But sometime after 1804 the Church received its new patron in statue form who did not apparently carry a cross and who may have been shown as he appears today standing upon the main altar jesticulating in a sign of welcome or possibly carrying his blossoming loaves of bread in his hands. At the same time that this new patron came, the Church received the effects of the passion side altar to the left, the large Judgment painting, the *Cristo Grande,* and the Dolores. This changed the iconographic pattern in the Church in accordance with another common paradigm found throughout the other missions of California. The statue of the Pilár formerly to the left, and even before that to the right, was now placed upon the main altar, rendering the pattern cross to birth, cross to

birth; that is, the cross outside of the church now stood opposite the new patron within (possibly holding flowering bread loaves) who stood above the statue of the Pilár holding the Infant Child just as the Judgment-Crucifix-Dolores on the left side altar stood opposite this statue of San José and Child. The infant is missing but was originally there, as San José's left hand makes clear. **100**

(Size: 4 feet.)

The two paintings recorded in the 1834 inventory on either side of this San José, a Purísima and another San José, have not as yet been found.

Photo 30 — Statue of the Dolores.

The Dolores described by Lillian Whaley in the Adobe Chapel in Old Town San Diego may now be seen in the side chapel originally dedicated to San Francisco and variously called the mortuary or Madonna chapel at San Luis Rey today. This statue was originally placed below the feet of the *Cristo Grande* (Photo 31) at San Diego Mission on the side altar to the left, as is suggested by the 1834 inventory of that Mission, a document of great importance, incidentally, because of the paucity of references to statues in San Diego Mission's annual reports even though they survive in comparatively large numbers. Only the year 1785 is missing, as well as the gap found in all mission records between 1796 and 1810.

In these annual reports, only the statue of the Pilár is mentioned in 1782. At San Luis Rey, Lanzoni clearly describes this San Diego Dolores, number 102, with "dark red dress with gold flower design and dark green mantle bordered in gold," and Father Dominic Gallardo of the same Mission clearly states that this "statue of the Sorrowful Mother" was among the "San Diego Mission articles." Still the copyist inserted the wrong Lanzoni number for identification, 107, which is a painting of the same subject, instead of 102. As said, the 1844 inventory of San Luis Rey listed only one statue that might be confused with these San Diego pieces, a Dolores. This statue at San Luis Rey was, however, too small, only 2 feet and 9 inches, to be this San Diego Dolores.

(Size: 3 feet and 8 inches. See Photos 3, 4, 5, and 11.)

The Cristo Grande

The only work of art among the group collected together in the vestibule of the Church of the Immaculate Conception in Old Town, San Diego, to be transferred to the care of the Mission San Luis Rey, which at the present time is no longer there, is the great and magnificently executed depiction of the Crucifixion, almost life size. Two important questions had to be answered, then, regarding this piece: first, Was this *Cristo* ever at San Luis Rey? and second, if not or if so, Where is it today? If all of the other works of art originally in the Vestibule of the Church of the Immaculate Conception in Old Town had been transferred north some thirty-five miles to San Luis Rey, probability would suggest that so too was this Cross.

Yet no one at that Mission recalled it from the photos shown (Photos 1, 1A and 11) although the present director, Brother Christian Rogan — to whom a personal sense of gratitude must be expressed for the many courtesies extended while this author was conducting research at Mission San Luis Rey — recalled that he had loaned a Crucifix of that size to a needy Franciscan community in Arizona. This, he recalled, originally hung in the dining room.

Others at the Mission, however, claimed that that piece was entirely modern. Furthermore, Lanzoni clearly made no reference to it in his long inventory of the Church and sacristy drawn up in the 1940's, whether modern or ancient. But in his 1954 commentary safely sequestered away behind locked doors in Room 63 with the rest of the historical material relating to the Mission, Father Dominic Gallardo distinctly stated that there was a "Crucifix behind the head table in the refectory," or dining room, which was from "San Diego Mission." This part of San Luis Rey, having been considered private, was not inventoried by Lanzoni, hence his complete failure to refer to the piece. Furthermore, in the second copy of the 1854 inventory, drawn up by Father Reynolds Flores, O.F.M., on February 7, 1955, a comment was attached to Father Dominic's statement to the effect that "the nails used in this work were gold nuggets. Two were stolen. The other had been darkened to hide it."

Perhaps the most striking photo taken of this Crucifix at any time may be found in a late 19th or early 20th Century view of the main altar of the Adobe Chapel of the Immaculate Conception in Old Town, presently in the Greene collection of the Los Angeles County Museum of Natural History. Since this glass plate is fully eight by ten inches and resolved the scene before it in the greatest detail, the entire Cross may be shown in addition to extreme enlargements of the nails in the hands and feet.

Photo 1A — Main Altar, Adobe Chapel, Old Town, San Diego, Showing Cristo Grande before Last Judgment Painting.

The gold nugget, clearly visible in the opened hand to the right, evokes scenes not of the brawling mining camps alone where it undoubtedly came from in the 1850's, but of other recollections equally compelling and rich if not far more strange. One can not help but recall the individual, sodden with whiskey, who broke into the Adobe Chapel two days before its dedication, in November of 1858, who was found "mounted on the top of the altar, embracing a figure of Christ on the Cross, which is very large, franticly *(sic)* imploring him to hear, and in his delirium he had broken off the arms and otherwise disfigured the body."

Could this "derelict" have had intentions less honorable than his drunken but devout state implied? If three nuggets were ever originally over the nail head of this *Cristo*, which certainly may be doubted, two of them probably went jingling out of the chapel in the pockets of this unhappy vagrant.

But such was San Diego itself in some ways in the roaring Fifties — happy, devout, unstable, unpredictable, even violent — a community of residents perhaps in greater truth who were coming to place more hope upon the cross ties of a railroad line than upon the Cross of this *Cristo Grande* in their small community Church, a people who were changing quickly but who were still capable of mingling devotion with delight by willingly decorating such images with wealth which then was easily come by, but who in their less serious moments just as willingly threw "gold and silver pieces and little bags of gold dust" at the flying feet of beautiful and talented *señoritas* to the thunderous applause of the crowd.

With the information supplied by the present director of Mission San Luis Rey, Brother Christian Rogan, O.F.M., and his assistant Brother Marion Alfonso, O.F.M., this beautiful *Cristo* was traced to a small Yaqui Indian community just southeast of Phoenix, Arizona.

Photo 31 — Cristo Grande of Mission San Diego, in Arizona Indian Village Chapel.

Presently, almost everything which can be imagined to have happened to this piece has in fact unhappily occurred. Of course, the nugget described as recently as 1955 is gone. The work itself has been temporarily (one certainly hopes temporarily) lost to the state; it has been re-painted almost beyond recognition, for which reason the brothers at San Luis Rey thought it to be a modern plaster of paris corpus. The original Cross has been removed and lost, yet in this photo anyone with an appreciative eye can see right through these glaring defects to the original quality of the work and imagine what this *Cristo* would look like if placed in the hands of a fully-qualified restorer. However, the first stage of restoration and appreciation itself is knowledge without the possession of which nothing, not even the essential origins of a culture, seems of any real value. But here in California, this lack of knowledge has not been a specific case with regard to mission period art, nor a condition relating to those individuals now at the various missions which now house these works, but in fact has remained a general case characteristic of California historiography. For that reason alone, the same kind of attention must be given to mission art today that was given to mission architecture at the turn of the century, or, as was said then of the buildings which composed those missions which we now treasure due to the effort of others, that art will simply disappear. Not mentioned by Lanzoni but specifically said to have come from Mission San Diego by Father Dominic Gallardo, O.F.M. (See Photos 1 and 11.)

Paintings

The paintings of Mission San Diego represent as complete a set as any to survive in California. They vary in size from the large eight-by-ten-foot canvas of the Judgment to the small three-by-two-and-a-half-foot depiction of San Diego, and of course in quality as well as age. They are in remarkable condition considering their history. Only two from the Mission have not been found, the small Immaculata and the San José of the same size.

The Presidio, so far as it may be judged, was a showcase of mission period art and for that reason possessed few of the less prestigious paintings. The large and beautifully executed Guadalupe, seen in Photos 3, 4, and 5, was perhaps its only canvas, and it alone of the entire collection once in the Adobe Chapel of the Immaculate Conception in Old Town has not been found. The items described and presented below, therefore, all came from the Mission up the Valley.

Paintings Today

The masterful quality of the *Cristo Grande*, shown in Photo 31 is perhaps only superseded in the entire mission chain by the beautiful Immaculata generally seen in the Adobe Chapel to its left (See Photos 1, 20, and 21) and the even more masterfully executed Judgment usually seen directly behind it in the same chapel. Still, however excellent the above Photos 31, 1A and 12 in black and white, the superb quality of San Diego's *Juicio Universal*, cannot be appreciated unless viewed in color. In the 1834 inventory of Mission San Diego this canvas was stated to be three varas high or eight feet, three inches. Today, without its modern frame, it stands seven feet, eight inches, but with it, eight feet, six inches, a remarkable correspondence. However, it is ten feet, three inches without and eleven feet, one inch with this frame in width. As in the Adobe Chapel, so too, in the Mission Church, this impressive canvas hung behind the above mentioned Crucifix on the side altar to the left.

Photo 32 — The Last Judgment of San Diego.
Photos 33 and 34 — Details of Last Judgment, The Damned, The Blessed.

No matter where the eye falls on this huge canvas it perceives figures in human form skill-fully drawn, not ten or twenty but literally hundreds — there are some 200 in whole or in part in heaven alone and unfortunately far more below. In the lower division, all are organized into radically diverging patterns of motion moving away from the center where stands the avenging angel of judgment. The work even at the slightest glance is clearly either itself a masterpiece or an excellent copy of one.

In fact, it is taken from the famous *Jugement Dernier* of Jean Cousin le Jeune. Completed in 1585 for the church of Vincennes in France, the relatively small original (4.76 feet x 4.66 feet) now in the Louvre, was first made known to the world outside of the small religious community which it served through an engraving by Piere de Jode the Elder. As was so common among Spanish-American artists, the creator of the San Diego Judgment worked from such an engraving as may be demonstrated by the fact that the color in the greatly enlarged copy in no way corresponds to that of the original. **101** At San Luis Rey Mission, this painting has never been seen generally by the public. Formerly located in the clerics' recreation room, it now hangs in the small semi-private chapel just to the west or left of the sanctuary, and for that reason was never mentioned by Lanzoni. Since noted authorities have suggested that this large painting was brought to San Luis Rey from Mexico by the Zacatecan fathers late in the 19th Century, it is important to examine Father Dominic's own remarks upon the matter. Leaving little doubt regarding its origin, he wrote, this "painting of 'The Last Judgment' found in the clerics' recreation room" was the property of "San Diego Mission."

(Size: 8 feet, 3 inches x 10 feet, 3 inches.) See Lillian Whaley's account of its title taken down in 1930, when it was still in Old Town San Diego. The reader also is referred to Photos 1 and 12.

The excellent quality of San Diego's Day of Doom perhaps may be most easily demonstrated by comparing it to a less competent copy of the same original engraving, presently located at Mission San Antonio de Padua but originally from Mission Santa Barbara in mission times.

Photo 35 — Last Judgment from Santa Barbara Mission.

This amateurish copy nevertheless has been called "the most interesting [painting] of the Mission [Santa Barbara] collection." **102**

The Stations of the Cross originally at San Diego, since they were merely prints, were not taken from Old Town apparently and have not been found as yet, although one of the two paintings of the Passion in frames listed in the San Diego 1834 inventory may be at San Luis Rey in a gilded frame.

Photo 36 — Painting of Our Lady of Light.

If records tell anything with certainty, they assert that the badly restored depiction of Our Lady of Light in Photo 36 is one of the oldest paintings of the San Diego mission period collection and, therefore, one of the oldest in the entire chain of twenty-one missions of California. It with only one other painting survived the 1775 San Diego revolt and fire. Its pre-restored state may be seen in the 1920's Photo 13. It is signed Luis S. Mena, whose work as said also appears at San Gabriel in the *Gloria*. The Lanzoni reference to this painting is not clear (115 or 265?), and so, therefore, is the subsequent inventory of Father Dominic which employs the Lanzoni numbering system. In any case, Father Dominic was apparently unaware that this painting came from San Diego Mission originally.

(Size: 61 inches x 61 inches. See Photos 1, 3, 11 and 13 and Lillian Whaley's significant description.)

Mission San Diego's First Three Patrons

Every mission in California was assigned a patron. Before its foundation a painting of this saint was commissioned in Mexico which, however, more often than not in the early period of the conquest of Alta California, failed to arrive at the appointed site for the founding ceremony. Such was the case at San Diego de Alcalá on July 16, 1769. Unknown to anyone in Upper California, a painting had been commissioned and stored aboard the packet boat the *San Antonio* when the ship made its first voyage to California from Cape San Lucas in 1769. On June 24, 1770, when this, the only reliable vessel of supply, was moored in Monterey Bay, Serra at the suggestion of Captain Juan Pérez came aboard and was directed to a *caxoncita* in the

cupboard of the ship's cabin put there over a year earlier. Inside he found three paintings of patrons, San Carlos for his own mission there at Monterey, just founded, San Buenaventura for a proposed but as yet unestablished site in the Channel area, and San Diego de Alcalá already founded the year before. The painting which Serra held in his hands may be seen in Photo 37.
103

Photo 37 — Earliest Painting of San Diego de Alcala.

All three of these were placed temporarily upon the altar at San Carlos Mission around the central statue of the Belén and Child.

Yet the intention was obvious, this last painting named was meant for Mission San Diego, already founded, where it was undoubtedly sent as soon as possible. The first record of its presence there at that Mission occurs in the *Inventario de Missión de San Diego de Alcalá*, 1777-1784, in the Bancroft Library, under the year 1777 where it is said to have been "very damaged as a result of the sacriligious mistreatment of the Indians in the year 1775" and where it is said to be about a vara and a quarter, (41¼ inches) tall. Although no museum photograph of this painting has as yet been found showing it in San Diego at any time, it seems to bear the scars of the 1775 fire and was said by Father Dominic of Mission San Luis Rey, where it may be found today in the sacristy, to have come specifically from Mission San Diego. It is listed with the correct Lanzoni number: "St. Diego with Angels (no. 238) in church sacristy."

(Size: internal measurements without frame: 36 inches x 28 inches.)

Before Serra embarked on the *San Carlos* on October 17, 1772, for Mexico on his crucial mission to the highest seat of imperial power in New Spain, Governor of California Pedro Fages, on the grounds of military security, had suggested that the already uncomfortably large Indian population at Mission San Diego, then still at its original location, be moved farther away from the Mission, to which the President of the missions responded coolly. However, while he was in Mexico City addressing the Viceroy, famine continued in the San Diego area unabated. When Serra's life-long companion

and the former President of the mission of Lower California, Francisco Palóu, arrived in San Diego in 1773, he initiated a search for more arable land which was found at the present Mission's site several miles up the Valley. With Serra's permission from Mexico, the Mission and its large Indian population was moved up the Valley. There is no documentary evidence to prove this, but the probability is that Serra, realizing in Mexico that there would be two chapels in San Diego as a result of that move, one at the new site of the Mission and another at the old at the Presidio, brought back with him in 1774 an additional depiction of the patron San Diego. The large two vara, or five and a half foot painting carried first by land and then by sea by this venerable and aged padre, may be seen in Photo 38.

Photo 38 — Largest Painting of San Diego de Alcala.

It is first mentioned in a Spanish document in the year 1777 in the 1777-1784 inventory and was specifically said to serve *"en el Presidio."* It was returned to the Mission, according to the same document, in 1790. Lanzoni number 149 where it is described unmistakably as a "large painting of 'St. Diego, holding a standing Cross and basket with bread and flowers'" — but unrecorded and uncommented upon by Father Dominic at Mission San Luis Rey.

(Size: 66 inches x 38 inches. See Photos 1 and 2.)

Photo 39 — Last Painting of San Diego de Alcala.

Before the largest painting of San Diego was returned to the Mission in 1790, San Diego Mission received another painting of its patron, reported in 1783 to be a vara and a half high (49.5 inches), that was of less somber tone than the larger one at the Presidio and its predecessor at the Mission. Lillian Whaley referred to this painting only in the briefest terms. It was called San Diego de Alcalá "in prevailing brown." Lanzoni's reference, No. 249, is even more brief: "S. Diego de Alcalá — small oil painting xviii cent., plain wood frame," while Father Dominic again remained silent, even though this painting may be seen in the choir in the old photos of Mission San Luis Rey's church interior.

(Size: 37.5 inches x 28 inches.)

The facts concerning the lost art treasures of San Diego are clear. Before a careful analysis was made of the subject, San Diego was considered a devastated parent mission district with little to nothing of its original art holdings, while in fact the opposite is the case: San Diego should be a haven for art historians. No other mission district can boast such historic treasures.

Notice the last three paintings enumerated.

They represent all of the original paintings of the patron of Mission San Diego, including the one damaged in the 1775 revolt and fire and subsequently repaired. (There are patches all over the back of this canvas.) But more generally, except for the one Franciscan santo, San Antonio de Padua, almost the entire invaluable collection has been found in addition to the most important images that once graced the walls of the Presidio Church. **104**

With such a high rate of retrieval, the art of both the Mission and Presidio Churches of San Diego may be shown as it actually appeared in the mission period.

*SKETCHES SHOW
ICONOGRAPHY
OF THE FIRST
CHRISTIAN CHURCHES
IN CALIFORNIA*

Unlike in a museum, a work of art in a mission was always placed in relationship to a whole pattern formed by other works of art. The large Crucifix, the Sorrowing Mother, and the Last Judgment went together as a stunning single unit at Mission San Diego to form the passion side altar to the left. But just as these three objects interrelated, so too did the three altars of the same church, where, above the main altar, San Francisco with his cross and San Antonio de Padua with his Child literally pointed to the side altars which elaborated upon these same emblems. At the Presidio, similar connecting art forms were employed which interlocked not only with liturgical plays performed there and elsewhere but also with the scholastic, philosophic, and scientific presuppositions of the Franciscan founders of the missions of California. Thus although each piece of art has been shown individually in color photograph, the presentation of these even more important interlocking iconographic relationships has been reserved for the following sketches constructed by the author himself to exact proportions.

Photo 41

Sketch of the passion side altar of Mission San Diego.
Located on the men's left side of the Mission Church,
this altar was decorated with the large Last Judgment scene,
the Cristo Grande, and the Dolores,
according to that mission's inventory for 1834.

Photo 43

*Sketch of the main altar of
Mission San Diego.
The Indian neophyte would have
seen San Francisco on the left,
generally, with his Crucifix in hand;
San Diego with his open arms of
welcome in the center above the
smaller statue of the Pilár, and
San Antonio de Padua, as generally
like San José, with his Infant Child.*

Photo 42

Sketch of the San José side altar of Mission San Diego.
Located on the women's right side of Mission Church, this altar,
aside from possessing a statue of its patron San José, was adorned
with two paintings, the Immaculata and another San José,
the entire display depicting birth or the family.

Photo 44

Sketch of the Pastorela *at the Presidio Church, San Diego. The nativity play seen by Alfred Robinson in 1829 is here shown for the first time with the art of the chapel in place, and it proves to be a dramatic mirror of the statue arrangement above the main altar where San Miguel, the hero of the play, was placed directly above the central statue of the Immaculata as her protector.*

Photo 44A

Detail of nativity play from preceding sketch.
Although unknown to Robinson, the nativity play Los Pastores enacted before his eyes was a mirror image of the art above the main altar of the Presidio Church. As generally throughout Mexico, San Miguel was almost certainly seen high above the star-crowned Immaculata, with his two assistants, San Gabriel with his lilies and San Rafael with his fish, on either side. In his military garb, this angel represented the military at the Presidio at San Diego as the protector of the Church, itself symbolized by the statue of the Immaculata at his feet. Therefore, this central angel was appropriately shown in the play in the act of protecting that same Institution from the forces of darkness.

San Diego's Mission Art as it Appeared to Indian Neophytes

The word "restoration" in one sense has a specific history both in Europe and in California. Its counterpart *"restoración"* still does not exist in the Spanish language generally which employs *"reparar"* or "repair" as its equivalent. No 18th Century Spanish dictionary may be shown to contain a word *(restoración* or *reparar)* that possesses the same meaning as the English term "restore" (actually of continental origin) especially as that word applies to a building. As a result, not one single Spanish-speaking person in California in the 18th and 19th Centuries may be shown to have possessed the notion implied by this word with respect to mission buildings themselves.

In fact, if anyone were allowed the questionable privilege of examining the interior of any Gothic cathedral in Europe in the same period, the 18th Century, Notre Dame de Paris as an example certainly, he would perhaps be shocked to discover the grotesque "improvements" visited upon such venerable structures by the more "advanced" taste of that age. The concept of restoration itself throughout Europe at large is an early to mid-19th Century invention that remained largely foreign to Spain and her possessions even throughout the remainder of that

century.

In California, a mission building was never "restored" but often "improved." That was what the Reverend Ciprian Rubio did to San Juan Bautista, San Buenaventura, and probably San Luis Obispo, which last building bore on its upper facade to the left: "CREATA MDCCLXXII" – and on its upper right: "REPARATA MDCCCLVII," the word "Repaired" here meaning "Improved." If this prelate were brought back from his grave today and shown that subsequently in this century almost all of his "improvements" had been torn out and replaced with imitations of the older, more primitive decorations from the mission period, he would simply at first become and then subsequently remain thoroughly confused.

The first individual in California to actively engage himself in the process of restoration in the contemporary sense of the word was, perhaps, the Reverend Joseph J. O'Keefe, a pioneer Anglo-American father whose work especially at San Luis Rey in the 1890's but also in some ways earlier at Santa Barbara was aimed, particularly with regard to the decorations in the Church, at restoring the former historic mission period style. From this period on, this essentially French conception was gradually developed in California perhaps most preeminently by Henry J. Downie at San Carlos. However, both in Europe and in California this work has been carried forth with the omission of one most important element, the restoration of the iconography of these venerable institutions. With regard to an essentially medieval society which employed visual art as one of its central if not its primary means of human communication, this has been an egregious oversight whose historical origin is, nevertheless, easily told.

The restoration of the Gothic cathedrals of France took place in the 19th Century under governmental, that is to say, under non-clerical jurisdictions led by Eugène Viollet-le-Duc whose training was essentially artistic and historic but whose personal sentiments were neither religious nor sociological. As he viewed the Cathedral at Paris, which he restored, as an aesthetic expression of the human spirit, given its individual character because it arose at a specific time in history, thus the entire Cathedral was conceived as a work of art. As a result of this perspective, the use of the religious art once in that great basilica was not thought relevant to his goals and was considered the concern of the prelate who happened to be in residence at the Cathedral site at the time. He did not conceive that the religious art may have had important non-religious functions which might provide a new tool for understanding the social matrix of the community which it served. Therefore, this intellectual heritage bequeathed by the French to the 20th Century was essentially secular in nature and artistic in temperament — and it has remained so. When it was brought to California by responsible Anglo-Americans of whom Reverend O'Keefe was perhaps the first active member, it still possessed this secular viewpoint despite O'Keefe's renowned clerical status.

Fortunately, where the Anglo-Americans failed in the area of mission preservation, specifically in relationship to mission art, the Spanish-American native Californians often succeeded gloriously. If the mission period church buildings, once their practical use had gone, seemed of little importance to the native Californians, this attitude was not similarly transferred to the art once housed in those institutions. This they valued both in a religious and in a historic sense. In contrast to the French conception of restoration which was secular-artistic and historic, the Spanish appreciation of a work of art was communicative and historic, not necessarily aesthetic at all.

In a communicative sense the work of art often fit into a larger iconographic pattern in the mission church. In this context, it often spoke to its viewer in a complex secular, philosophic, even metaphysical, and certainly in a religious sense. Historically even a mediocre piece of mission art may nevertheless have been highly prized because it was employed by Serra or some other important dignitary on this or that equally important historic occasion. That was why the three original paintings of San Diego de Alcalá were preserved. By this process, each statue or painting at a mission was eventually clothed in a mantle of historic associations which gave the community a sense of historic continuity.

A better understanding of this essentially Hispanic sense of a work of mission art's value may be had if it is approached with the same discipline associated with the Anglo-American concept of restoration. This indeed has been the goal of this work: the restoration of works of art to their historic setting even if the mission period church is no longer in existence. This actually may be done with such accuracy that the reader may accomplish what no other Anglo-American has been able to do from the very first to visit these California shores in the 1820's, that is, to examine the iconographic holdings of those two historic Church buildings long since destroyed with some understanding of what he is seeing before his very eyes.

THE ICONOGRAPHY OF MISSION SAN DIEGO

Since the actual appearance of the objects referred to by the 1834 inventory of the Mission San Diego's Adobe Church is now known, they may be placed with the assistance of the skills of an artist in the specific places which they originally occupied when the inventory was drawn up at the close of the mission period.

Photo 41 — Sketch of Side Altar to Left, Mission San Diego.

In this sketch is shown an association that may be found employed generally throughout all California mission art. The Dolores was made to stand below such a Christ-on-the-Cross and as such may be called or classified a cross-santa. Just as invariably, the Last Judgment was associated with such mournful figures as is demonstrated clearly in Photo 1 of the interior of the Adobe Chapel, where the *Cristo* was placed in front of this huge painting, as it was before in the Mission, even though the patroness of the Chapel was the Immaculate Conception, seen in that photograph to the left. However, on December 8, this Cross was taken away, the "birth-santa" or patrona in the form of the Immaculata placed in the defining or commanding central position, and as Miss Whaley was careful to point out, the painting of the Judgment was thereupon considered inappropriate and therefore carefully covered in lieu of being physically replaced. The flower-bedecked image of the Immaculata in the center of the altar, therefore, defined the general character of the entire decoration.

In just that manner such images were set apart permanently on their respective altars in the Mission, with the central, defining image determining the character of the entire decoration. Furthermore, the *dolorosa* or mournful or cross images were generally placed on the left where the Indian men stood in the Mission Church, the *gloriosa* ones to the right where the Indian women stood. The Mission did include a small painting of the Immaculata (to demonstrate the point being made here), and as expected it was placed with the statue of San José, whose robe, as may be seen in Photo 29, was bedecked with flowers and in whose arms would have been seen the Infant Child. Thus this art clearly helped define the roles of the respective sexes of the neophyte Indians in the same way as it had for centuries in Europe. The philosophic, metaphysical, and quite factual consideration of death and that for which it stood as a symbol, thought-directed away from the world, was associated with men; beauty, floral exuberance and the joys of perception general-ly, family, and birth with women. These are associations basic to Western man.

Photo 42 — Sketch of Altar of San Jose.

If such a large statue of the Immaculata had been at the Mission and had been placed on one of the two side altars, that is, it could not have been placed with the Passion side altar but with its opposite, which as said, was done, however, with a small painting of the same subject. In the sketch shown in Photo 42 San José is seen dressed appropriately for such a genetic or birthside identification, his gown covered with flowers and, as generally throughout the rest of the missions, with the Infant in his arms. Clearly the small paintings of the Purísima and a second San José upon the wall above this defining statue conform to and actually represent a "family" grouping above the heads of the Indian women on that side, very much as the Cross image of San Diego and the painting of Our Lady of Light and Birth were used in the Adobe Chapel in Old Town — for a purpose. Besides this "behavioral" implication of this placement, which gave definition to the masculine and feminine members of the mission community unheard of in the pre-conquest state of Indian tribal life, there were the obvious metaphysical implications of this division: the Logos or principle of Reason on the left leaving the world (or going away from the senses) and on the right entering it (or directing the mind or care and attention toward things and people in that world).

Photo 43 — Sketch of San Diego Mission's Main Altar.

Here on the main altar, as shown, it is possible to feel the presence of the mission spirit, with the three Franciscan santos in their niches stretching across the sanctuary wall, and yet surrounding the central Virgin and Child "seemingly as pleased as could be" as Serra remarked of the very first altar arrangement of this kind in California involving such a number of images. **105** And yet again the Church would probably be divided according to the same principle, the cross santo to the left (San Francisco is always shown holding a Crucifix), the birth-santo to the right (San Antonio de Padua, like San José, is always shown with the Infant).

But perhaps the greatest immediate value is the insight that it may give us into Alfred Robinson's brief description of the interior of the Presidio Church on the evening of December 24, *la noche buena*, in the year 1829 when the *Pastorela* was performed there under the direction of the now familiar Don José Antonio Estudillo. With the information now in our possession, we are almost capable of seeing this event as it actually occurred before Robinson's own eyes, thereby making it possible to look over his shoulder and point out the most significant details which he omitted and even correct observations which he made that have misled historians of the mission period from that day to this.

THE PRESIDIO CHURCH IN 1829

San Diego on the flat below Presidio Hill in 1829 when Alfred Robinson first took up lodging there was not a decade old and if any small rural community ever did summon up the wearisomeness of small town life, this one certainly did, as this young visitor from Boston recounted in his own words:

The family in which I now resided at St. Diego consisted of the old lady Dominguez, Don José Antonio Estudillo and his wife, Doña Victoria, with two children, and three servants. My first week's residence proved rather dull, and I found it necessary to make frequent hunting excursions in the neighborhood, with an occasional ride to our dépôt at "Hide Park" in order to wear away the time, and break up the monotony of our little village. **106**

Occupied in the relatively new hide and tallow trade on the California coast, this young New Englander in addition had to bear up with the inconveniences of temporary lodgings at the Estudillo House, located on the east side of the town square, in order to conduct his trade.

My new lodging unfortunately had no direct communication with the street, except by a small window, so that my customers were compelled to pass through the *sala* and a sleeping apartment, ere they could get access to my place of business.

Any form of amusement under these circum-stances, even practical jokes, seemed welcome, especially if they backfired on the perpetrator as was the case with the distinguished *Señor* Don Lugo. Having prepared a cigarette loaded with gunpowder for Robinson who fortunately did not select it from the pack during the evening's conversation, *Señor* Lugo returned to his quarters quite forgetting the entire matter. However, while lying sleepless that night in bed next to "his fair *esposa*," he unwittingly selected the cigarette intended for Robinson and almost blew "the better part of his moustache" away to say nothing of the effect this sudden explosion and effusion of smoke had upon the quietly reclining *señora*.

Two years before Robinson's visit, San Diego seemed equally unimpressive to the distinguished French captain of *Le Héros*, Auguste Bernard du Hautcilly, who would later publish his plaintive impressions in his *Voyage autour du monde* in Paris in 1834-1835.

Of all the places visited during our sojourn in California ..., the Presidio of San Diego was the saddest. Built on the slope of an arid hill, it is without regular form. It is a collection of houses rendered even more bleak by the brown color of the coarsely made bricks which compose them ... Below the Presidio on a sandy plain, thirty or forty houses of poor appearance are dispersed with some poorly cultivated gardens.

Without newspapers or any other means of public communication, this quiet and peaceful hamlet at the foot of the hill composed more realistically of some twenty adobe houses still looked to the Presidio Hill, its parent, for entertainment. As chance would have it during Bernard du Hautcilly's stay, the citizens of Old Town were drawn there by a bull fight, which the captain of the 370-ton French trader described magnificently:

The Church of the Presidio which forms one of the sides of the interior court, is constructed on a hill with a very steep slope in such a manner that one of the ends of the roof is supported on the hillside while the other is elevated very nearly forty feet above the ground. The bull, more disposed to flight than combat, startled by the cries of the spectators and threatened by the confinement, not finding any means of escape, was driven back near the place where the roof of the church seemed to become a part of the mountain. He had no further avenue left for retreat, and a spring of two feet in height placed him on the flattened [aplati] roof of the chapel where everyone was expecting to see a sudden descent into the sanctuary as he advanced himself, breaking through the tiles where he stepped now with one leg, now with the other. Finally, stumbling as he went, he arrived at the most elevated part of the roof before having recognized the imminence of his danger that he then seemed to comprehend with a new dread. He attempted nevertheless to turn around and repeat his steps, but with this movement, he slipped and fell into the courtyard along with a heap of débris and in the middle of a cloud of dust. One can hardly believe the clamorous glee that the cruel death of this poor animal excited in the descendants of the Spaniards.

Robinson was not blessed with such fortune, staying as he did in Old Town in the middle of a sunny and uneventful winter. Bull fights he undoubtedly saw, but the event which he witnessed in his *Life in California* of more interest to him and to us occurred within the Presidio Church itself, for in this Adobe Chapel on special days of the year, various forms of public entertainment would be provided as Robinson himself made abundantly clear:

It was nearly time for the religious festival of "la noche buena," and he [Don José Antonio Estudillo, the man primarily responsible in later years for saving the art in both the presidio and mission churches with whom Robinson lodged] directed the customary exhibition of the "pastores." They were rehearsing night after night, till at length Christmas arrived, and I had an opportunity of beholding the ceremony of midnight mass and the subsequent performance. **107**

In such a community this was a much looked for and long remembered event.

At an early hour illuminations commenced, fireworks were set off, and all was rejoicing. The church bells rang merrily, and long before the time of mass the pathways leading to the Presidio were enlivened by crowds hurrying to devotion. I accompanied Don José Antonio who procured for me a stand where I could see distinctly everything that took place. **108**

Now for the first time since these words were written in 1829, it is known what Robinson actually saw in the Church before the ceremonies began, or where the bull seen by du Hautcilly almost came crashing through along

with half of the tile and reed roofing overhead.

Whether a man of special privilege or not, the young New Englander would have been placed on the left-hand side of the Church interior, perhaps somewhere midway between the tall facade and the caverned out sanctuary and main altar, near the entrance to the mortuary side chapel on the left. For as Robinson himself asserted elsewhere, such a placement by sex was the practice generally throughout Spanish California.**109** On the right he would have seen the women of the village, on the other side of the Church; over there, perhaps underneath the painting of the Guadalupe, *Doña* Lugo with the explosion perhaps still ringing in her ears, over there, with a retinue of women about her, *Doña* Victoria Estudillo, etc. And as he looked around, his attention would have fallen upon the awesome Virgin above the main altar, standing upon her crescent moon and crowned so majestically. High above her head there would have been the three archangels in military costume, San Gabriel above to the left, San Miguel even higher directly above the Virgin, and San Rafael at the same level as San Gabriel to the right. Of course, this young man's New England background would not allow him to assimilate these dominating iconographic motifs of the Presidio Church as a single unit. For him each of these statues would remain unclearly defined because of their absolute strangeness (for which reason they would neither be recalled nor described). And above all, they would certainly not be seen for what they were, as they would be understood for instance by everyone else in the Church, as the mirror image of the play that was about to begin. In order to have understood this, Robinson would have to have conceived not merely the San Miguel and the two other archangels as a single group but more importantly these three in connection with the crowned Virgin below standing on her crescent moon.

All of these graceful images were intended to be seen as a single unit drawn from a single passage in the last book of the New Testament, the twelfth chapter of the *Apocalypse*. For in that text, as in the play to follow based in part upon it, San Miguel is mentioned by name as the protector of this woman standing on her crescent moon symbolic of the Church in its sublunar state. If this candlelit altarpiece was not seen in this way, neither would the play which was drawn from the same passage of scripture. 110

The Mass commenced, Padre Vicente de Oliva [from the mission] officiated [he who would later leave the church art in Don José Estudillo's charge], and at the conclusion of the mysterious "sacrificio" he produced a small image representing the infant Saviour, which he held in his hands for all who chose to approach and kiss.111

Here was suggested another central theme of the play to follow which Robinson would miss. The audience in the Church came to this tiny image of the new-born Christ Child at mass as the shepherds or *pastores* in the play would be shown coming to Him at Bethlehem. Therefore, the shepherds in the play were intended to be identified with the individuals in the audience of the Church who watched them. This relationship would be developed into comedic caricature that would provide much of the entertainment to follow; specific individuals or types in the audience would be imitated in the play and yet this would be accomplished with a point.

After this, the tinkling of the guitar was heard without, the body of the church was cleared, and immediately commenced the harmonious sounds of a choir of voices. The characters entered in procession, adorned with appropriate costume, and bearing banners. There were six females representing shepherdesses, three men and a boy. One of the men personated Lucifer, one a hermit, and the other Bartolo, a lazy vagabond, whilst the boy represented the archangel Gabriel. 112

Here was Robinson's first and most far-reaching error, his identification of this angel of the *Pastores* as San Gabriel, for this would later be repeated by Walter Colton and again and again by the major Anglo-American authorities who addressed themselves to this subject specifically, until Edith Webb, as has been pointed out elsewhere,113 could conclude in her encyclopedic work published in 1952 entitled *Indian Life at the Old Missions* that "accounts differ somewhat as to some of the characters in the play, but always there were the archangel Gabriel, Satan or El Diablo ..." etc. The facts are, Robinson did not see San Gabriel in this

production of the *Pastores* at all, nor had anyone else ever seen him in such a performance as the protagonist.114

The angel actually was San Miguel. Robinson would have avoided this error had he only looked at the altarpiece before which the play took place and recognized that central angel high above the Virgin as San Miguel — or if he had known about the passage in the *Apocalypse* where a dragon or a Devil attacked the Virgin (hence the presence of El Diablo in the play), who was saved by San Miguel, not San Gabriel. Not having any knowledge of this text of the *Apocalypse* which accounted for the biblical origin of the play, Robinson would fail to mention this last book of the New Testament, upon which so much before his eyes was based, just as he had failed to describe in any way the statues above the main altar drawn from the same source. That was why as well he and others who would follow him would consider the characters drawn from the *Apocalypse* superfluous "additions" to the biblical account of the nativity.

The story of their performance is partially drawn from the Bible, and commences with the angel's appearance to the shepherds, his account of the birth of our Saviour, and exhortation to them to repair to the scene of the manger. Lucifer appears among them, and endeavors to prevent the prosecution of their journey. His influences and temptations are about to succeed, when Gabriel [*sic*] again appears and frustrates their effect. A dialogue is then carried on of considerable length relative to the attributes of the Diety, which ends in the submission of Satan. The whole is interspersed with songs and incidents that seem better adapted to the stage than a church. 115

More detail may now be added to this account concerning the costumes and actual action of the play.116

The "lazy old shepherd" Bartolo was dressed "in skins" and went about the Church "carrying a stout staff and cow bells" when he was not deposited "upon the floor ... asleep." The hermit was dressed as a Padre, "in a coarse grey gown and cowl and sandals with rosary and corn cob cross suspended from a cord around the waist." The two older and four younger "shepherdesses formed two lines facing each other, Bartolo ... upon the floor at the end of one line ..., the hermit ... at the end of the other facing him." The two older women heading each line would have been closest to the Manger located before the main altar near the sanctuary railing perhaps elevated on a small stage, the hermit and Bartolo for comic relief closest to the audience in the body of the Church. "The two older ladies" nearest the manger "were in black," the "four younger ones" with hair curled "with a poker iron" were in different colors, with beautiful "silk embroidered shawls heavily fringed ... Each ... carried a heavy staff with crooks and flowers at the top, and a gift for the child."

At a signal, the two old ladies began the singing in which [the others] joined, keeping time with [their] staves upon the floor. The simple words of the song bespoke a general desire to pay a visit to the new born king. Each verse was repeated and [they] marched around following [their] leaders to [their] original positions and always keeping time with [their] staves. The shepherdesses are distressed about Bartolo who will not rouse himself and follow them. They plead in vain. He sings drowsily in response but sinks to sleep again. Finally they attack him in a body. They sing to him with loud determination, take hold of him [and bring him] to his feet, after which he staggers along behind the rest. Bartolo and the hermit furnish the amusement both for the players and audience by keeping up a series of pranks and jokes.

About the middle of the play Lucifer suddenly enters, a Spanish gentleman in black suit, red sash and hideous false face. He rants and rails. He represents the difficulties of the journey to the shepherdesses. They become intimidated and are about to abandon their project and return to their flocks when an angel, in gauzy draperies and wings suddenly appears, sword in hand. A colloquy ensues which results in a clash of weapons in which Lucifer is defeated and overthrown. Both then withdraw and the shepherds continue their journey. After much singing the manger is reached. This was represented by a deep basket, softly lined in which the Babe was laid, a much treasured little saint belonging to the old church. The gifts are presented, Bartolo staggering up with the one he has brought. The songs of presentation, the hymns of praise are strikingly simple and pretty. After the farewell hymns the shepherds take their leave and the play is ended.117

To Robinson (and Colton along with many more to follow them) the hermit, Bartolo, El Diablo, and the angel's dramatic conflict were "grotesque appendages"118 to the Lukean account of the nativity. But if the angel were San

Miguel and not San Gabriel as Robinson and all those who followed him claimed, then both St. Michael and the Devil would have been entirely scriptural since they, and in fact the entire dramatic conflict of the play, would have been drawn from the same text of the Apocalypse.

Photos 44 and 44A — Sketch of Presidio Performance of Pastores.

The narration describing the costumes and characters in greater detail was taken from an account of the play recalled meticulously by Lillian Whaley who acted in it herself. This was included in her unpublished but copyrighted account of life in Old Town. So great was the influence of Robinson's original error regarding his identity of the play's angel as San Gabriel that, it will be noticed in the account she presented, intended for the public if not for publication, Miss Whaley nowhere offers the actual identity of this central figure of the little drama. Immediately after the conclusion of her personal account, Miss Whaley makes reference to the most authoritative figure then living on the subject of Californiana, Theodore Hittell, giving the title of his recently published History of California by name. In the second volume, on page 501, may be found a description of this play taken almost directly word for word from Robinson, which gives the identification of the angel again as San Gabriel. Thus with all the weight of published authority standing against her, Miss Whaley in her account intended for the public refrained from identifying the angel of the Pastores correctly for the San Diego area, that is, as San Miguel, which she knew him to be. But in her private Memoir not intended for publication and also presently at the Whaley House in Old Town, San Diego, she did not hesitate to clarify this point.

There she wrote on page 2 concerning this same performance:

Don Jose Maria Estudillo [the director and son of Don José Antonio who directed the performance seen by Robinson] represented Lucifer, in black suit and red sash. His young son represented the archangel Michael by whom he, Lucifer, was defeated in a sword contest.

Also:

There were four young girls and two older women representing the shepherdesses. The older women were Doña Luz Marron Estudillo, wife of Don Jose Maria, and Doña Lugarda Machado. The three other girls [i.e., besides Lillian Whaley herself] were the daughters of Don José Maria and Doña Luz. ... The angel — St. Michael — was Luz's little son, whom they called "Chumalia." He had on long white cotton stockings, and wings on his back.[119]

With this angel's identification established,[120] a more critical comparison is invited between the statues above the main altar forming the principal part of the sanctuary design of the Presidio Church and this play conducted before them. The question is, why were the hermit and Bartolo included, aside from the fact that they were obviously intended to exemplify the theme suggested at the beginning of the performance, when everyone in the Church came to the sanctuary altar rail to the Infant as the shepherds would do in Bethlehem? This made these shepherds, including such characters as the lazy Bartolo and the ascetic padre, a comic looking glass for some of the members of the audience who watched them. But was there something more? In fact, this question is related to another.

On the altar, San Miguel stood above the mystic Virgin who was shown as the woman of the *Apocalypse*, crowned with twelve stars with the large crescent moon at her feet. In the same text of that book which formed the basis both of the play and of the altarpiece, this woman is attacked by the Devil in the form of a dragon. In the play a group of shepherds led by an eremitical gray-robed padre is attacked by this demon. Why the discrepancy? Why wasn't the Virgin attacked in the play as she was in the Apocalyptic text? This problem is solved completely when the scholastic interpretation of this twelfth chapter is understood:

the woman on the crescent moon attacked by the dragon or Devil is seen both as the Virgin at the Nativity (the woman in the *Apocalypse* gives birth to a child) thus connecting this passage to a play about the Nativity, and as of old she is seen as a symbol of the Church on Earth (the Devil could hardly wage war on the Church in Heaven). Therefore, while the Virgin above the main altar symbolized, these shepherds and their padre represented this same Church on Earth and stood one the equivalent of the other. The answer to both questions then — why the extra characters and why were the shepherds attacked, etc. — is the same; the shepherds and padre represented the Church on Earth, just as the woman on the crescent moon represented the Church on Earth.

But things which are equal to the same thing are equal to each other. If this Virgin representing the Church, who was visibly protected above the main altar by San Miguel, was equal to these shepherds and padre in the play, who were also protected by this angel, then the people in the audience, who were equal to these shepherds, must have conceived themselves under the protection of that same angel. Of course, anyone should know that Michael is the protector of the Church generally and should be able to deduce from the above what Serra stated as fact as early as 1779, that this same angel was the specific protector of the missions of California themselves. What fascinates and even strikes one as utterly ingenious is the way the scholastic presuppositions of a Serra, or any one of a number of his followers in the missions of California, gave this view scientific and even cosmological support, if not iconographically in the Presidio Chapel in San Diego then certainly elsewhere in other missions along the Coast and more importantly in manuscripts both from Spain and the mission archives in California in the hand of these same padres.

BELIEFS BEHIND THE SYMBOLS AND DRAMAS OF THE MISSION ERA

The value of the recovery of the lost art treasures of San Diego's Mission and Presidio Churches does not end with the knowledge of their original placement as the Indian neophytes and Spanish Californians saw them, nor with our understanding of the relationship between this art and a pleasant, festive liturgical play like *Los Pastores* performed there every Christmas season. Behind this secular version of the nativity drama lay a more serious intent, actually acted out under the direction of the padres at other missions with the identical iconographic arrangement as was found at the Presidio of San Diego. Even an Indian neophyte recently in from the hills — who understood no more or less about these art forms than we do today — nevertheless would find the entire scholastic universe presented right before his eyes. Key passages from the last Book of the New Testament, the *Apocalypse* of John, were interpreted in accordance with Aristotelian physics and cosmology. This historical origin of synchronization of Biblical text and scientific pretext has never before been published.

Photo 45 SOUTHWEST MUSEUM, LOS ANGELES (PASADENA)

A New Knight photograph of sanctuary of Mission San Antonio de Padua.
Taken circa 1889 by a salon photographer from San Francisco,
this formerly unpublished view of the interior reveals the same
sanctuary arrangement seen by Alfred Robinson in 1829 on Presidio Hill:
a protector San Miguel is seen above a central Purísima Concepción,
here not only placed in but made a part of the entire scholastic universe.

Photo 46

The Nativity Play Los Pastores *performed at*
Mission San Antonio de Padua, as sketched by Lyle Gallon.
Under the direction of the padres, this liturgical drama would
have been given symbols more clearly drawn from the Apocalypse and
the complete repository of scholastic thought.
The Virgin on the crescent moon above the altar would symbolize
the sublunar world, the star-filled arch the "fixed stars," and
in between, San Miguel with the Sun and Moon on his chest serving
as the Captain of the planetary spheres.
The planetary Intelligences are even more clearly represented
in the play by the seven star angels.

Photo 47

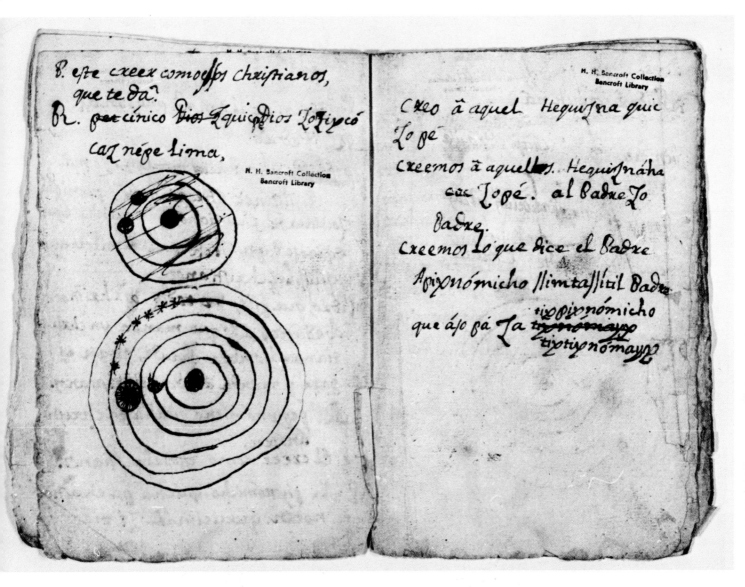

Sketch of the Scholastic Universe from Mission San Antonio de Padua,
completed by one of its founding fathers,
Fray Buenaventura Sitjar, O.F.M., in 1773.
In this manuscript, half in Spanish and half in the Indian language
of that Mission, is shown the same scholastic universe seen in the
Mission's sanctuary and the reconstructed Nativity play,
characteristic of the thought of Aquinas and Buenaventura of the
13th Century and of the founder of the missions of California,
Fray Junípero Serra.

Mission Art — Vestige of a Past that Lingered in California

The need to preserve the art treasures of the Mission and Presidio Churches of San Diego may be justified on their merit as works of art alone, although they certainly possess other value. We have called these heretofore lost artifacts of Spanish mission culture "treasures" because they afford us the opportunity of reconstructing what has been up to this point in time a virtually lost world view that bears directly upon the development of Western Civilization in its scholastic period — a world view that has become lost not only to historians of California but to scholars of Western Civilization generally. However, at San Diego, because nothing survives of the actual church and sanctuary decorations in either of its two mission period churches, we are left with nothing but a glimmer of this lost world. Fortunately there are alternatives.

Alfred Robinson in later years witnessed a second performance of the *Pastores* in Santa Barbara put on by mission Indians and judged this second production far superior to the one seen earlier at the Presidio at San Diego.121 Although exceptionally little is known about such mission plays, yet by the most careful and most scrupulous collection of data, added to by later accounts which seem at first sight unreliable, it is possible to reconstruct a production of this Nativity play in a mission church interior about which a great deal is known. The result of connecting such mission art with its founders' known philosophic and scientific views is the complete recovery of the scholastic paradigm which in turn forces us to agree with Robinson's own judgment concerning the superiority of such a mission presentation of the play. With the padres themselves directing the performance, the curious 20th Century observer is placed that much closer to the candlelight of scholastic thought which the dramatizations at San Diego emitted only in a pleasant yet somewhat dimmed glow, for in the mission performances the Apocalyptic allusions were drawn more fully and the scholastic cosmology and science applied more systematically.

About three months after witnessing the production of the *Pastores* at San Diego, Robinson concluded his business in Old Town and sailed upon the ship the *Brookline* for Monterey from where he had to "repair" immediately to the Mission of Santa Barbara by horseback. He was soon brought "to the neat little Mission of St. Antonio, which was the first mark of civilization"

Photo 48

This near life-size statue of
San Francisco de Asís originally stood
probably to the left or gospel side of its
mate, the centrally placed statue of
San Diego, above the main altar of
San Diego Mission.
This important piece was found with the
help of Father David Temple, O.F.M.,
Guardian of Mission Santa Barbara,
who received it in the 1950's from
Mrs. Irene Heylman Robinson and her
late brother, George F. Heylman, Jr.
According to Mrs. Robinson, their mother,
Mrs. Mary Smith Heylmann, received it
before her marriage to Mr. Heylmann, Sr.
in 1909 from the Lopez family whose
house, the Casa de Lopez, received it
temporarily on loan in the early 1950's.
According to Mr. Edward and
Mrs. Robinson, the santo was found by
the Lopez family in a covered chicken coop
just below the Presidio near the
Serra palms with other artifacts from
the Mission, including a badly damaged
second statue, doubtlessly the as-yet-unfound
San Antonio de Padua.
This tradition both of the Robinsons
believe corresponded to the remark of
Francis Whaley made in the mid-1870's
regarding an adobe structure which housed
such mission artifacts located east of the
Bandini House, which according to the
Robinsons, would be in the direction
of the Presidio.

The work is presently located in the
private Friars' Chapel of Mission
San Miguel, just above
Paso Robles, California.

(Size: 48 inches.)

that he had encountered in that wide-open country among the Santa Lucia Mountains on the second day of his journey out of Monterey. The Mission, founded in 1771, was "built of brick, with an arched corridor similar to the other missions. … Everything was in the most perfect order; the Indians cleanly and well dressed, the apartments tidy, the workshops, granaries, and store-houses comfortable and in good keeping." **122** Had Robinson the opportunity of witnessing a performance of the *Pastores* in this Mission Church as he had at the Presidio at the conclusion of the previous year, even he might have been struck by the intent of the entire production.

In this Church at that time he would have seen the same iconographic arrangement as he had found at the Presidio Church of San Diego, but here we are more capable of knowing exactly what else he saw in the way of church and sanctuary design. As at the Presidio, an Immaculate Conception would have been seen above the main altar of the Church of the Mission of San Antonio and above her head as well, another statue of San Miguel holding a balance scale in his left hand and a tall standard of the Cross on his right. As at San Diego Mission, here too would have been seen a Passion side altar to the left and another opposite to the right devoted to a San José and Child below a painting of the Guadalupe. Furthermore, this Virgin above the main altar clearly symbolized the Church on Earth because her statue was carefully placed right in the center of the star-filled arch representing the fixed stars, making her by her placement the symbol of the central Earth. Moreover, above the Virgin and below the starry arch, an angel was placed just as carefully in the planetary position in this scholastic universe, who was appropriately decorated with the Sun and the Moon, on his star-filled tunic of blue.

Photo 45 — Knight Photo of San Antonio Church Interior.

This arrangement was not the same as the use of an occasional star or sparkler to decorate or enliven a scene. This was a systematic use of symbols designed to represent a specific cosmological point of view.

But according to the play and the text of the *Apocalypse* from which the former and this altarpiece design were derived, this angel was supposed to help this Virgin here so clearly shown as the Church in its terrestrial or sublunar state. How could this angel, so closely associated by position with the planets, help effect that goal? Had Robinson come to ask such a question at San Antonio he might have fallen upon one of the central but more often than not unstated principles of scholastic thought to which Padre Buenaventura Sitjar, one of the founding fathers of San Antonio Mission; Padre Junípero Serra, the founder of the missions of California; Duns Scotus, whom Serra followed in these matters; Aquinas, and San Buenaventura, to mention but a few, would and did unhesitatingly assent:

These [angels] according to the philosophers move the celestial bodies [i.e., the planets], and according to the theologians, rule the universe in accordance with … the work of reparation.**123**

This work of reparation on Earth, of course, was carried out by the human institution for which the Virgin stood, the Church. And where on Earth was this work of reclaiming man from his fallen state being carried out more clearly than here in these twenty-one missions of California?

If these statements about the planetary function of such angels were merely sound hypotheses, then their correspondence to the remarks about the meaning of such art, whether at the Presidio and Mission of San Diego, or at the Mission of San Antonio, would remain only moderately relevant. But the implications of this angel's placement at San Antonio — that such angels were believed to control the planets — is not mere theory; it is absolute historic fact. That is, we are dealing here with the recovery, not merely of some invaluable works of art from the mission period but with the rediscovery of a real world view that rarely in the entire history of man has had such a close correspondence between thought, art, and social structure.

Sitjar, a founding father of Mission San Antonio, states it as clearly as anyone else:

The stars move because the Cosmos is composed

of the same Spheres which certain angels move, to whom God had given these charges, and since they are spirits incapable of fatigue, they move them continuously without tiring.124

Or as Serra put it in his philosophical lectures given in far-off Spain:

I say ... that the Spheres are not moved by themselves but by certain Intelligences or Angels.125

Into this scholastic world at San Antonio Mission came a different kind of a *Pastores* if we may trust the account of Joseph Smeaton Chase. There, not less than seven star-topped angels, the full number of the planets, would have been seen dressed in white and carrying candles in accordance with the Apocalyptic text.

As at San Diego, according to author Chase, after midnight mass in this rude Adobe Mission Church at San Antonio Mission the *Pastorela* would have begun.

First enters a handsome, smooth-faced young Indian in a tunic of blue bespangled with gilt stars [just as the angel high above the altar], with a similar larger star fastened with wire above his forehead. ... Then appears a figure at the sight of which the women press back and hold the children against their knees: a tall cadaverous personage, face grotesquely painted in blue, white, and yellow, with two small goat's horns projecting from his forehead and wearing a sleeveless coat which like his bare arms and legs is emblazoned with red flames. ... "El Diablo! Satanás!" is whispered shudderingly. Following him comes a clown-like fellow in fantastic garb, moping and mowing and panting as if crazy. He is known as Bartolo. ... Last enter six girls in white robes reaching to the knees, carrying candles and wearing white, veil-like headcovering, each with a small gilt star. They are plainly angels ... but instead of remaining with the other characters in the midst of the church, these go to where a low platform has been built, just outside of the altar rail [at San Antonio, directly underneath the star-filled arch representing the "fixed stars"] on which is an object that is covered with a large cloth [the Virgin and Child]. The angels take their stand, three and three, on each side of the platform.126

San Miguel,127 portrayed by the young smooth-faced Indian boy in his tunic of "blue bespangled with gilt stars," naturally defeats El Diablo, shown as a pre-conquest Indian in

the body paint colors of the Salinan tribe of this mission, and at the conclusion —

Cross in hand, now leads the shepherds towards the star [high over the crib], Bartolo and the Devil following, and as they reach the platform, the Archangel draws the veil aside and reveals a rude, straw-filled manger, in which is seen the image of the Holy Child, while at the end is a small statue of the Virgin. Then comes the closing tableau, the Archangel, the angels with lighted candles, the shepherd, and Bartolo grouped about the manger, *El Diablo* in the background, and the star shining over all.128

Photo 46 — Sketch of Closing Tableau by Lyle Gallon.

The source for this version of the *Pastores* and its meaning in terms of scholastic cosmology is equally clear. These seven star angels like the characters of San Miguel and El Diablo were unmistakably drawn from the *Apocalypse*.

And being turned, I saw seven golden candlesticks, and in the midst of the seven candlesticks one like unto the Son of man. ... And He held in His right hand seven stars. ... The seven stars are the angels of the seven churches, and the seven candlesticks ... are the seven churches. 129

The cosmological treatment given this passage in the play also may be shown to have been widespread throughout the scholastic world. According to the last great Spanish commentator on this text,

the seven angels — among whom are named Michael, Gabriel and Raphael — [are set] over the seven planets. ... And if we delete ... the names Michael, Gabriel, etc., to this same opinion many Peripatectics may be said to subscribe, who allot to each sphere a single Intelligence, and so particular angels to the seven planets.130

Such was the meaning of the closing tableau at San Antonio, where the angels in white and San Miguel, completing the number of seven star-angels, stood underneath the star-filled arch which represented the fixed stars. There in visible form was a cross-section of the entire scholastic universe. 131

To be able to stand before this conclusion of the *Pastores* at Mission San Antonio de Padua here in California and comprehend its relevance to the scholastic thought of the founders of that Mission and of the founder of the missions of California, Fray Junípero Serra, to say nothing of the great scholastic doctors of the 13th and 14th Centuries is infinitely more meaningful than the fascinating feast of the *Fariseos* described and witnessed in the first chapter of this book in far-off Arizona. Because, here in this small Mission in California, indirectly at least, one may see through a glass darkly the entire social matrix of Western Man in its formative stage actually at work.

Emile Mâle at the beginning of this century spoke of the Gothic cathedral as "medieval thought in visible form, with no essential element lacking."[132] Unlike the Presidio at San Diego where the Church itself does not survive in photos and where the documents and manuscripts relating to that Church and its builders are entirely lacking at this point, at San Antonio this Mâlean hypothesis may be checked and completely confirmed.

But did the gray-robed padres of that Mission actually teach this scholastic world view to the Indians in their charge, as the above sanctuary design would imply alone, even if no credit at all were given to the *Pastores* recounted by Chase? The answer is, yes, without any doubt they did, as the following document from that Mission clearly demonstrates. [133]

Photo 47 — 1773 MS in Sitjar's hand, Bancroft Library.

The sketch shown in Photo 47 is, however, only the skeletal remains of the living thought that once had a visible form in the art and life of the Mission. Such too is the story of the lost art treasures of the Mission and Presidio of San Diego. They complement exactly a new understanding of the art found in the entire mission chain in California and funnel the mind to a deeper understanding of the Middle Ages. Their Presidio Church is gone, but they are the very flesh of its existence and so await patiently its resurrection.

Acknowledgements

This extended piece of research, lasting as it did for so many years and bearing recklessly on without concern or care for funding, was made possible by my wife, Rita Nolan. There are also many others whom I wish to thank: certainly everyone at the Los Angeles County Museum of Natural History, in history — especially Dr. Harry Kelsey but also Curator of History William Mason and John Cahoon; certainly everyone there in photography as well, especially Lawrence Reynolds for his exceptionally creative work with the difficult black and white museum photographs; surely everyone at Mission San Luis Rey today, Edith, Brother Marion, but especially the present Director Brother Christian Rogan, O.F.M., but also one thinks of the past, especially of Father Dominic Gallardo, O.F.M. Also, there is everyone at Santa Barbara Mission, surely the renowned Guardian and Saint Francis authority Father David but also the acting archivist working under Father Guest, Bogden Deresiewicz, medievalist, whose own work will shortly be in print. In San Diego itself there are those at the Mission, Father Joseph Halter and Phyllis especially, as well as everyone at the Whaley House in Old Town, especially June Reading (but her husband Jim as well) whose generous help with the Whaley documents proved so valuable; also several people at the University of San Diego, but particularly Dr. Ray Brandes for his help with the MS initially. One could go on — at Copley Books, Jean Bradford, or at the old location of the *Union* in Old Town, Dick Yale, etc. However it may appear, a work of this kind could not possibly have been attempted except for the generosity and cooperation of others. I think of people like Larry Booth, then with the Title Insurance and Trust Co. in San Diego and especially of Dolores Narramen in Los Angeles. I would like to complete this list with the names of two individuals whose work has had a personal and direct influence on this author, the Reverend Father Maynard Geiger, O.F.M., lamented, and his life-long friend, Henry J. Downie.

1. Herbert Eugene Bolton, *Font's Complete Diary* (Berkeley, Ca., 1931), p. 213; Zephyrin Engelhardt, *San Diego Mission* (San Francisco, 1920), p. 72.

2. Francisco Palóu, *Relación histórica de la vida y apostólicas taréas del venerable Padre Fray Junípero Serra* (Mexico, 1787), p. 87, henceforth *Vida*; Maynard J. Geiger, *Palóu's Life of Fray Junípero Serra* (Washington, D.C., 1955), p. 79.

3. Alfred Robinson, *Life in California* (New Edition, San Francisco, 1897), pp. 31 and especially 262-263 where Robinson supplements the earlier description of San Diego.

4. Richard F. Pourade, *The History of San Diego, III: The Silver Dons* (San Diego, 1966), p. 40.

5. Engelhardt, *San Diego Mission*, p. 243. This may have been the last important ceremony performed in the Presidio Church, for on December 30, 1841, we are told in the baptismal register, that the ceremony of baptism was performed "in the chapel of the port of San Diego," Engelhardt, ibid., p. 285. However, see Paul Ezell's article, "The Excavation Program at the San Diego Presidio" in *The Journal of San Diego History*, vol. xxii, no. 4 (Fall 1976), p. 18, where this "chapel" is identified with the Presidio Church.

6. "The grave in which Henry Delano Fitch was buried in 1849 was broken through the tile floor [of the Presidio Church] at a time when the walls of the building had so far disintegrated that their precise location could no longer be discerned," whereas for such burials when the Church was still in use, "the floor tiles had been replaced after the burials," "A Landscape of the Past," *The Journal of San Diego History*, vol. xiv, no. 4 (Oct. 1968), p. 29.

7. William E. Smythe, *History of San Diego 1542-1908* (San Diego, 1908), I, p. 241.

8. "San Diego in 1854," *The Masterkey*, vol. xv, no. 6, Nov., 1941, p. 239.

9. There is a collection of uncatalogued documents in the De La Guerra and Mary K. Bowman boxes of the History Division of the Los Angeles County Museum of Natural History, two thirds of which may be found in the Santa Barbara Mission Archives in the De La Guerra Collection but one third of which, clearly De La Guerra family letters and the like may not be found there. Most of these are hastily translated from the Spanish but one, the Gillespie deposition originally in English and doubtlessly in the Bancroft, is a close copy to which attention is drawn here. Box I, "Gillespie, Archibald H. — San Francisco, February 25, 1868. Deposition, Heirs of the Estate of Santiago Argüello vs the United States."

10. Ibid.

11. Engelhardt, *San Diego Mission*, p. 255, Gillespie, loc. cit.

12. Engelhardt, ibid., p. 255.

13. Ibid., p. 257.

14. Ibid., p. 258.

15. Ibid., p. 257.

16. Ibid., p. 259.

17. Ibid.

18. Ibid., p. 261.

19. Ibid., p. 343.

20. Marjorie Tisdale Wolcott, *Pioneer Notes from the Diaries of Judge Benjamin Hayes 1849-1875* (Los Angeles, 1929), p. 295. Henceforth, *Pioneer Notes*.

21. Ibid.

22. *San Diego Mission Burial Register, 1850-58*, no. 47, Dec. 27, 1853.

23. "San Diego in 1854," loc. cit.

24. *San Diego Herald*, vol. VII, no. 20, Oct. 31, 1857, p. 2, col. 1.

25. Ibid., vol. VIII, no. 12, Oct. 4, 1858, p. 2, col. 2.

26. *Memoirs* of Lillian C. Whaley, typewritten MS in the Whaley House, Old Town, San Diego, p. 49; Mrs. James E. Reading, "Estudillo, One of the Early Homes," *Butterfield Express*, vol. 1, no. 2, Nov. 1962, p. 10.

27. Hazel Wood Waterman, "The Restoration of a Landmark (Casa Estudillo)," p. 10; unpublished MS in Serra Museum, San Diego. Not all seven of these bells came from the Mission. According to the 1834 inventory, two large bells were then at the Mission, one medium size, two small and a sixth even smaller. A bell or some bells were in the Presidio Church in 1829 when Robinson was there as he remarks about the jubilant air of the town's people as Christmas Eve approached in that year: "The church bells rang out merrily, and long before the time of mass the pathways leading to the Presidio were enlivened by crowds hurrying to devotion." op. cit., p. 78.

28. *Herald*, I, 20, Oct. 9, 1851, p. 2.

29. Benjamin Hayes, *Emigrant Notes and Scrap Books, 1850-1874*, quote taken from Richard F. Pourade, *The Silver Dons*, p. 39.

30. *Memoirs* of Lillian Whaley, p. 49; Reading, loc. cit. This description appears to contain a basic contradiction, since the *northeast* corner of the Estudillo House would be the one closest to the Bandini House in the front, while the compartment is said to exit on to San Diego Avenue which could only be achieved if the room were located in the southwest corner of the same facade. This is made even more complex when it is understood that the street along the front more commonly known Mason Street was apparently also known as San Diego Street and that in fact a door did exit out into San Diego Street from the northwest corner of the Estudillo House. Therefore one can not discern by Miss Whaley's remark alone which room or corner was intended, whether she meant the *south*west exiting on to San Diego Avenue or northwest exiting on to San Diego *Street*. However, since the door in the corner closest to the Bandini House facing the Plaza and exiting out onto San Diego *Street* does not appear in the Powell sketches of San Diego in 1850 even though it may be seen in the earliest photographs in the 1870's, we may assume that it was cut "through the walls of the western side of the house" facing the plaza on June 30, 1869, as José G. Estudillo states himself in his reply to a partition and title suit directed by Rosario E. de Ferrer against Victoria Estudillo et al., case no. 198 filed Jan. 11, 1869, located in box 15027 in the San Diego County Records Center on Overland Avenue, with the reply filed July 9, 1869. San Diego Street, not listed in the Couts and Poole Maps for San Diego, was taken from Thomas L. Scharf's map of Old Town drawn up in 1976.

31. H.M.T. Powell, *The Santa Fé Trail to California 1849-1852*, ed. Douglas S. Watson (San Francisco, 1931) opp. p. 186 for the Powell sketch of San Diego. There are two

other copies at the Huntington. Neither in these sketches nor in the Couts map does the Estudillo House appear to have a corral. Floods periodically inundated Old Town in 1855, when the unfinished church was damaged, and especially in 1862, when both the Bandini and Estudillo Houses lost their corrals (Ensworth to Thomas Whaley, Jan. 26, 1862, MS in the Whaley House, Old Town San Diego). The corral for the latter was erected in November of 1867 according to the above reply to a partition suit of José G. Estudillo. In the Powell sketches the peal of bells and stand supporting them appear to be across San Diego Avenue next to the Courthouse. These facts, however, seem at odds with the statement quoted above made by Ames who speaks of these bells in 1857 already erected on a "gallows . . . in a corral near the Plaza."

32. Teacher's Report to the Public School, District [of San Diego], no. 1, Aug. 31, 1864, signed Victoria P. Magee teacher, Serra Museum. For the "Size and Fitness of the School Room," Mrs. Magee wrote: "Adobe room 40 x 20 feet, ceiling 12 feet high." The type of school was primary. The thirty-ninth child on Mrs. Magee's roster, age 8, was Lucy Brown, who along with her parents, Mr. and Mrs. Captain John Brown, and Mr. and Mrs. Magee lived in the Estudillo House at the time. Many years later Mrs. Lucy Brown Wentworth recalled her experiences in that room and house. "In 1864 we were living in the Estudillo House (in the part nearest the Bandini House). My family consisted of my mother Martina de Villar, my father Capt. John Brown, my sister Ellen, John, Philip, Fransisco (sic) [and] my self — Lucy and baby brother Francisco Brown. We used part of the house; Mrs. Victoria Pedrorena Maggiee (sic) lived in the other half (on S.D. Avenue); she taught Public school in the room that had been used for a church." MS in Serra Museum. A sketch published by Clyde Trudell but originally submitted in the famous 1856 habeas corpus case involving Lucy's teacher, then Victoria Pedrorena Hammond (case no. 602, box no. 15033, Records Center), shows a floorplan many have identified with this House. This was the year Benjamin Hayes informs us that the Chapel of Old Town was located in the Estudillo House. In the plan, however, there is no such room indicated. As may be determined by reading the 1856 case itself where it is stated twelve separate times by name, the house in question discussed throughout the entire proceedings and represented in the attached floor plan is not the Estudillo but the Aguírre House which faced onto San Diego Avenue, not onto the Plaza. This explains not merely the absence of the large chapel in the sketch but the obvious contradictions implicit in the Estudillo House identification. For at the trial, Henry Magee would testify that "Mrs. Sutherland occupies the room at the corner nearest the Courthouse" to which statement was submitted the sketch in question, showing this room to be that farthest to the left as one faces the house front, where the Courthouse is shown even farther to the left. If the sketch were the Estudillo House, the Bandini House would have gained a new and previously unknown function in San Diego's colorful history, etc. In the same testimony, Magee states the facts exactly: "The Family of Aguirre and of Mrs. Estudillo are separate and distinct, although they live in the same building. The house belongs to Aguirre, and Mrs. Estudillo and family are residing there . . . Don Antonio

[Aguírre] and wife occupy a sleeping room by themselves. The two families all eat together. Mrs. Sutherland occupies the room at the corner nearest the Courthouse . . . Victoria de Pedrorena generally occupied Mrs. Sutherland's room and slept with Mrs. Sutherland or the girls . . . I was there almost every day." The only way that the Estudillo House could have been intended in the light of the above testimony repeated twelve times — and this has been assumed — was if Aguírre in fact owned the Estudillo House facing the Plaza as well as his own, making it possible to refer to the Estudillo House as the Aguírre one. However, Aguírre never did own the Estudillo House as the list of the holdings of this land baron prove (Rosario de Ferrer vs. Manuel Ferrer, July 13, 1868, case 185, box 15027, Records Center) along with the complete record of this property's ownership provided by Brandt Burghall of the Title Insurance and Trust Co. of San Diego and confirmed in the Recorder's Office. The certainty of these facts is of value not merely to clarify the ambiguity regarding the existence and location of the chapel in the Estudillo House but to point to this sketch, however roughly drawn, as a valuable tool should the Aguírre House site, now of course occupied by another building, be excavated and the house itself actually restored. Here and only here, so far as this author knows, are the subdivisions of the rooms of this famous dwelling indicated, which when coupled with photographs of the exterior should reveal the precise location of the wall foundations both within and without. A sense of gratitude must be expressed for the help given in this matter in this note to Marion Brissette of San Diego's Law Library, whose work there over the years relating to these complex court cases has become of such great value.

33. The width of this apartment, 20 feet, necessitated that this room be located in the front of the Estudillo House since the interior width of the rooms in the two wings did not exceed 14.5 feet. The front apartments on either side of the central double doors were both approximately 19.5 feet wide, and neither the one to the northwest to the left of those central doors nor that to the right to the southwest exceeded 35 feet in length.

34. Richard F. Pourade in his *The Silver Dons* and others independently have placed this lot 88 "on the other side of the river where the padres' road to Mission San Diego intersected with El Camino Real," ibid., pp. 163 - 164, following possibly the Charles H. Poole map (and other undisclosed sources) which shows Old Town with two block 88's, one as shown on the earlier Couts map, four blocks east of the Estudillo House along San Diego Avenue and the other about the same distance west approximately along the same San Diego Avenue line, however, across the river. However, all records of the transaction (*Deed Book B*, pp. 154 - 155, and the *Minutes of the Common Council of the City of San Diego, June 17, 1850 to March 16, 1868*, pp. 58 - 59 of typewritten MS in Serra Museum) specifically designate block 88 "as indicated upon the plat of City Lots of San Diego as drawn by Lieut. Cave J. Couts" whose map contains only one block 88 to the east of the Estudillo House from which site, moreover, all records of ownership of the property may be traced to the present day, as has been done by the Title Insurance and Trust Co. of San Diego.

35. "Probably" is a word with wide implications. The facts as they are known today would imply that the

108

Church begun in 1851 in San Diego was almost certainly left unfinished — but again, the word "almost" must be employed. On June 28, 1852, the year following the cornerstone laying, for instance, Father Holbein had "to take up another contribution to pay for roofing those barren walls" (*Herald*, II, no. 3, June 28, 1852). Clearly the church was still unfinished in that year. Such was still the case in the following year 1853 when Lieut. Derby first moved to San Diego, as he noted in the August 26 issue of the *Daily Alta California:* the "Catholic church [in San Diego] . . . meets in a private residence." On the sixth day of the same month and year in the San Diego *Herald* was noted "that the lumber [presumably for roofing] has arrived from Santa Cruz, to finish the new Catholic church in this city, and that the work is to be pushed ahead with vigor, in order to have the house [but not the church?] ready for occupancy by the time Padre [Holbein] returns from Lower California." In the following month, however, the *Herald* announced a surprise: "The Rev. Padre Juan Holbein [was going] to leave San Diego and return to Germany" (III, no. 32, Sept. 17, 1853, p. 3.) What effect this news had upon the plan to finish the church so expeditiously is not known. However, just five months after Father Holbein last signed a register in September of 1854, that is, on January 6, 1855, the *Herald* reported a disaster: "During the recent rains the adobe wall on the north side of the New Catholic Church, became so undermined by washing of the foundation, that on New Year's night, about half of it fell with a crash that could be heard all over Town." Moreover, the *Herald* editor moralized: "The building would have been finished long since" had it not been for Father Holbein's anti-Masonic sentiments which alienated many of the non-Catholic citizens of the community. Editor Ames' words "would have been finished long since" did imply that the structure had never been completed. Furthermore, no dedication record for this church has as yet been found. Still caution is suggested even though the *Herald* speaks of a "chapel" in Old Town, San Diego, as late as Dec. 3, 1853 ("The attendance at the Catholic chapel is full," III, 43, Dec. 3, p. 2) because in the following week the editor changed that word "chapel" to "church" (Dec. 8 "is a sort of religious affair, and is piously observed by services in the church, bull fights in the plaza, and balls in the evening," III, 44, Dec. 10, p. 2) and because, of course, a small church could be properly referred to as a chapel, the very kind of reference apparently employed in the following week to the same church-chapel when it was remarked that this "sacred edifice" (a term hardly appropriate for a room-chapel in a private home) was used as "the judges' stand during the sack-race," III, 45, Dec. 17, p. 2. There is no doubt about 1853, Derby's testimony specifically referring to a church in a "private residence" for that year. And the 1851 Adobe Church building, finished or unfinished, fell in on the first day of 1855. Therefore, late 1853 and all of 1854 force us to say that it is almost certainly true that the 1851 Church was never completed, for there is no evidence for this period. Incidentally, as has been pointed out by others, in the *Minutes of the Common Council* and in *Deed Book B* in the places mentioned above, the grant of lot 1, block 88 was made on the condition that a church be built there. If one were not built, the gift would "become absolutely null

and void and the ownership . . . revert to the City," which is precisely what happened in 1855 after the Church was destroyed, *Book E*, pp. 260 and 371.

36. *Pioneer Notes*, p. 121; for manuscript reference, *Emigrant Notes*, the Bancroft C-E62 pt 1 photo, p. 114; Journal — 1856, p. 113. Judge Hayes says Rumor has been circulating "for some time." If the Holbein church had been completed, this rumor could not have been circulating for more than a year, since January of the previous year when the church building collapsed.

37. *Deed Book B*, p. 154; *Minutes . . .*, p. 58.

38. Padre Holbein employs the word "church" repeatedly and specifically in the *Libro de Matrimonios 1850-1858* for San Diego throughout his entire stay there even when it is known with certainty that no such church existed in Old Town. Page 10, no. 2, for example, starts, "*El día 12 de Febrero 1850, en la Iglesia de este pueblo de San Diego,*" and such specific designations "*en la Iglesia*" continue right up to p. 35, Sept. 27, 1854, to the last ceremony bearing the signature of Father Holbein. Thereafter, perhaps more realistically, the visiting fathers almost invariably wrote "*en la capella del pueblo de San Diego,*" and so as well in the *Libro de Bautismos 1846-1856* after 1854.

39. *Herald*, IV, 41, Jan. 6, 1855.

40. Much of the following text relies heavily upon exceptionally important documents presently in the Whaley House, Old Town, San Diego. A personal and professional expression of gratitude must be expressed to Mrs. June Reading for having edited, re-typed, and shared these many manuscripts with this author.

41. P. 10.

42. The fourteen-page MS is in the hand of Frank Whaley in the Whaley House, p. 10.

43. MS in Whaley House, typewritten, p. 29.

44. Captain Brown's daughter Lucy wrote: "My father built that little adobe church on San Diego avenue (*sic*). He built it as a house for his family. He had a bowling alley there at one time but there were not very many people here and he didn't do very well with the bowling alley. He deeded the place to Don Jose Aguirre, who gave it to the people as a church." *Typewritten Notes of Lucy Brown Wentworth*, Serra Museum. This account conforms with county records where we are informed that Aguirre paid Brown $350.00 for lot 1 of block 26 according to the Couts map, Bk. 1, p. 187. Aguirre transferred the same to Bishop Amat for the sum of five dollars on Nov. 23, 1858, ibid., p. 275.

45. *Herald*, VIII, no. 17, Nov. 27, 1858, p. 2.

46. Ibid.

47. *Ynventario general de las existencias de la Mision de Sn Diego echo el dia 20 de Febrero de 1834*, p. 4, SBMA (Santa Barbara Mission Archives). Significantly, according to the 1844 inventory of the next mission to the north of San Diego, San Luis Rey did not possess a similar passion size Crucifix.

48. *Libro de Bautismos*, 1859, p. 19; Marleen Brasefield, *La Casita de Dios*, p. 13, unpublished manuscript in Serra Museum, Old Town, San Diego.

49. *Herald*, III, no. 44, Dec. 10, 1853, p. 2.

50. Lillian Whaley, *California's Oldest Town — 1769-1893*, copyright 1893, pp. 21 - 23, unpublished typewritten MS in Whaley House, Old Town, San Diego.

51. *Herald*, III, no. 44, Dec. 10, 1853, p. 2.

52. Ibid., no. 5, Dec. 4, 1852, p. 2. Powell, *Santa Fé Trail,*

p. 187.

53. Lillian Whaley, *California's Oldest Town*, p. 20, the last bullfight in Old Town having taken place on Dec. 8, 1869: San Diego *Union*, IV, no. 34, May 30, 1872, p. 4, but see also ibid., IV, no. 10, Dec. 14, 1871, p. 4.

54. Ibid., p. 54, in chapter entitled "The 8th of December, 1893 — Old Town."

55. *Herald*, III, no. 5, Dec. 4, 1852, p. 2.

56. Ibid., V, no. 18, Sept. 1, 1855, p. 2.

57. Antonine Tibesar, *Writings of Junípero Serra* (Washington, D.C., 1955), III, 241.

58. Ibid., p. 165.

59. The original text of Palóu's *Noticias de la Nueva California* in its author's own hand has been lost but a photographic copy of the Figueroa handwritten copy may be found in the Santa Barbara Mission Archives, taken from vol. XX, *Sección de Historia*, AGN (Archivo General de la Nación) Mexico City. This in the 1850's was rendered into print, and in San Francisco in 1874 under the editorship of the Historical Society of California, reproduced into four volumes of Spanish text edited by Doyle. These were translated critically into four volumes of English by Herbert Eugene Bolton, *Historical Memoirs of New California* (Berkeley, Ca., 1926). The lists contained in these documents may be compared to another in the hand of Francisco Palóu brought to my attention by Curator of History William Mason of the Los Angeles County Museum of Natural History where it may be found in photo duplicate under the title: *Razon de los ornamentos, Vasos Sagrados, y Utensilios de Yglesia y Sachristia que se han Sacado de las Missiones de Californias para las Missiones de Monterey por orden del Señor Visitador General Don Joséf de Galvez ... 8 de Mayo de 1773*, pp. 12 - 16 of the *Expediente del Año de 1774, Californias, no. 43 GG, no. 6: Sobre el reintegro de los Ganados, ornamentos, y vassos Sagrados que sacaron de las Missiones de la antigua California para las de la Nueva de Sn. Diego y Monterrey* (Sección: Provincias Internas, vol. 211, ff. 10 - 24, AGN).

60. These may be found in the *Noticias* (San Francisco, 1874) and in the *Historical Memoirs*, I, pp. 43 - 49 and 54 - 59 respectively, and in the *Razon de los ornamentos*, etc. pp. 12 - 15. However, the latter contradicts the former regarding the size of the statue of the Immaculata, the actual Figueroa handwritten text of the *Noticias* reading "*una Ymagen de la Purisima Concepcion de vara y media de alta con Corona de Plata*" (I, p. 16) while the *Razon* reads in full: "*Una Ymagen de la Virgen, de Marfil chiquita; Una dicha de San Philipe de Jesus; Otra dicha, como de media vara de la Purisima Concepcion con coronita de Plata*" (p. 15). The inventories in the *Noticias* make no mention of the San Philipe or the ivory statue of the Virgin which may have been lost at sea on the *San José*. The reference to the Concepción as only half a vara tall was not a slip, for the crown was said to be a *coronita*. I suspect the *Razon* even though in Palóu's own hand because of the excitement engendered at San Diego in 1775 at its loss, which would not have been occasioned had the statue been so small, and because of the crescent moon of such large dimensions under the Immaculata of the Presidio which shall be discussed more fully below.

61. *Noticias* (San Francisco, 1874), I, p. 44.

62. Tibesar, *Serra Writings*, I, p. 189.

63. Palóu, *Vida*, p. 131. Geiger calls this Madonna at San Diego a painting, *Palóu's Life*, p. 119. Palóu's text reads,

"*Imagen de nuestra Señora la Virgen con el Niño Jesus en los brazos.*" This accords exactly with what is known of the statue then in the mission period and with what may be seen of it today. For a description of this Virgin lactando, see *San José, La Iglesia más antigua en Puerto Rico*, [Guide Book to], pp. 20 - 22 where accounts from the 17th to the present century are presented showing this Virgin breast feeding the Niño.

64. Bolton translation, p. 199. Spanish text taken from Font's original in the John Carter Brown Library, Brown University: *Diario a Monterrey*.

65. Mission San Diego had a painting of its patron before the Mission was founded, although no one in Upper California knew that fact. Being small, about three and one half feet in length and probably half that wide, this canvas was rolled up with two others of the same approximate size in a *caxoncita* and placed to one side in one of the cupboards of the ship's cabin in the packet boat the *San Antonio* when it first departed from Cape San Lucas in 1769. There it remained until accidentally discovered the following year in June of 1770 (Tibesar, I, p. 187). This painting was a vara and a quarter (3' 6") in length, according to the 1777 annual report in the Libro . . . de esta Mission de San Diego de Alcalá or as listed in the Robert E. Cowan Collection of the Bancroft, the *Iventario de Misión de San Diego de Alcalá, 1777-1784*, C-C 237 covering the period from July 28, 1777, when Lasuén came, to 1784 when he left. I would like to thank Dr. Ray Brandes of the University of San Diego for putting a copy of this important document in my hands. This small painting was said to have been damaged considerably by "the sacriligious manhandling of the Indians in the year 1775." Ibid. Nevertheless, while a larger two vara (5'5") depiction of the patron probably brought from Mexico in 1774 by Serra would serve at the Presidio Chapel, this "original," well-tarnished depiction of that Mission's saint, as the same 1777 report and the 1783 inventory (SBMA) both record, would continue to serve at the Mission until 1783 when a new painting of the same subject, 1.5 varas or 4 feet square, was received and "placed upon the main altar" (Annual Report, 1783, SBMA). In the book of annual reports for the Mission of San Diego, 1777-1784, in the Cowan Collection in the Bancroft, at the conclusion of the section dealing with the church and sacristy, the following note is appended:

> Nota dia 28 de Mayo de 1790 bolvieron del Presidio [un] Caliz y quadro de San Diego ... Todo lo qual debolvio Don José Zúñiga teniente Comandante del Presidio.

> Note on the 28th day of May 1790 a chalice and a painting of San Diego [the two vara one] were returned from the Presidio, all of which Don José Zúñiga returned, being the *Comandante* of the Presidio.

66. This letter was in the California Archives, P.S.P., IX, pp. 583 - 586, according to Hittell's reference, *History of California* (San Francisco, 1897), I, p. 537, note 1, which collection, of course, was lost to the page in the San Francisco earthquake and fire. Bancroft's "agents" examined it when compiling their invaluable synopsis of these documents, recorded the date as Feb. 10, 1790 and nothing more, considering its contents without essential interest. Hittell fortunately thought differently but copied it apparently only in translation unfortunately (the original document is not in the Sutro Library), his entire paraphrase intending to prove that not all men in California had blackened the picture with outright criminal behavior; some excelled:

> One of these [noble acts] is observed in an exquisite letter written in February, 1790, by José de Zúñiga, the comandante of San Diego, to his mother Doña Maria Barbara Martinez. Addressing her in the most affectionate but at the same time respectful terms as his "Estimably dear little mother and madam," he complained that it had been days since he had heard from her or from Don Bonifacio; and in his anxiety he prayed God it was not on account of want of good health on their part: as for himself, he was strong and robust. He had the pleasure of informing her that in the course of the past year a beautiful church had been commenced at the presidio under his charge and an image in honor of the pure and immaculate conception provided for it; that he had been instrumental in accomplishing the work and had himself personally labored as a mason and as a carpenter and had painted the whole with his own hands; and he thanked God that she would thus see that her son, who had done things that were evil, was now zealous in doing things that were good. He went on to say that he sent her fifty dollars as a present for herself and his Señor father, and ten dollars to be expended on carmine, vermilion and other painting materials which he required and which he desired should be forwarded to him. He further requested if she had any comedies to spare, notwithstanding they might be old ones, that she would send them; for, though he had but little time to read, yet they would serve to divert him in those solitudes; and he would be obliged for any histories of the Most Holy Virgin and especially any works on the mystery of the pure and immaculate conception . . .

Concluding by requesting some "garden and flower seeds" and remaining "her most affectionate son," Zúñiga reveals a great deal of importance about the San Diego Presidio at the time and an equal amount about himself which explains why he was so well thought of by the Indians, padres, and soldiers of the San Diego area.

67. The Nuestra Señora del Pilár, *chica*, was first mentioned in 1777 (Inventario . . . 1777-1784, the Bancroft, C-C 237) in the Mission's book of records but not in the annual report of that year (SBMA) which last would have implied that it was a new arrival. Despite the statement made in the 1776 annual report (SBMA) that "all images were lost, except a painting of San Diego and one of Our Lady of Light," known to be in error since the Infant once in the arms of San José (see 1777-1784 inventory) survived, this statue of the Pilár may also have come from Baja California in 1769 or at least from Mexico in the pre-revolt mission period, for the 1777-1784 inventory specifically states for the year 1777 that "a statue of Nuestra Señora del Pilár and the prints of the Via Crucis [the latter known to have been in the pre-revolt mission church according to Serra's 1774 annual report of Mission San Diego, Tibesar, II, p. 226] were being guarded in a container until the [mission] church was [re-]built where they would be placed." The new mission site up the river had been called Nipaguay by the Indians (Tibesar, II, p. 225), but the Spanish had named it *Nuestra Señora del Pilár* (Palóu, *Historical Memoirs*, I, p. 308). According to the 1782 report (SBMA), this statue's altar was placed then on the epistle side. Later, when the Church had two side altars, the evidence

suggests that in the early 1800's this Virgin was moved to the gospel side altar and later still between 1804 and 1810, as dealt with more specifically elsewhere, to the main altar.

68. This small altar Crucifix was half a vara tall (1′4.5″), 1783 inventory.

69. Two paintings, each one vara (2′9″), 1779 report (SBMA) and 1777-1784 and 1783 inventories.

70. This could be any one of the three paintings of San Diego once at the Mission; see note 65 above.

71. These paper prints are undoubtedly those reported by Serra in 1774 (Tibesar, II, p. 226) and by Lasuén in 1777 (in the 1777-1784 inventory) and in 1783 (inventory).

72. This rare painting which predated the 1775 revolt, according to the report of that year filed late, in the early part of the following year 1776, was old even then (see also the 1783 inventory). There was also a very small painting of Our Lady of Light at Mission San Diego, mentioned for the first time in the 1783 inventory. The older was the larger mentioned as such in the 1777-1784 inventory when it was also stored, as said already of the Pilár and Vía Crucis.

73. Came in 1786 (SBMA); both were paintings.

74. Arrived in 1779 (SBMA), a vara and a quarter (3′5.25″) showing John the Baptist baptizing Jesus. It should be noted, finally, that except for the Pilár, no statues of any significance were recorded in the extant annual reports of San Diego Mission.

75. Annual report for 1779 (SBMA and Bancroft).

76. *Herald*, VIII, no. 17, Nov. 27, 1858, p. 2.

77. Paul Ezell, "The Excavation Program at the San Diego Presidio," *The Journal of San Diego History*, XXII, no. 4, pp. 1 and 7 for a photograph and a plan and pp. 13 - 14 for the text.

78. Such a hole may be seen, as shall be discussed more fully later, in the San Diego de Alcalá in the Serra Museum on Presidio Hill; see Arthur Frederick Ide's article, "San Diego, the Saint and the City," *The Journal of San Diego History*, XXII, no. 4, p. 21 for a photo of this three-quarters santo.

79. Lillian Whaley, *California's Oldest Town*, pp. 16 - 19.

80. Ibid., pp. 54 - 56.

81. Churches in Old Town San Diego had a difficult time getting completed in the 19th Century. Holbein, starting his adobe structure in 1851, apparently did not finish the work before it was undermined by a rain storm and flood in 1855. The Adobe Chapel, formerly already completed as a home and actually smaller in its interior dimensions than the large compartment or hall in the Estudillo House, surely was intended as a temporary affair only. Accordingly, Father Ubach almost within the decade of the dedication of the Adobe Chapel in November of 1858 planned a new brick church for Old Town, whose cornerstone was laid in July of 1869 in commemoration of the 100th anniversary of the foundation of the City and Mission of San Diego. Tragedy, the great fire of 1872 and the exodus of people from Old to New Town San Diego, rendered its completion impractical. Its gothic walls were left half raised without a roof until 1914 when they were finally removed and the site cleared for the present Church of the Immaculate Conception, completed in 1917 but not dedicated until 1919. For the best exposition of this subject to date, Sister Marleen Brasefield, *La Casita de Dios*, 1973, MS in Serra Museum.

82. Brasefield, *La Casita de Dios,* p. 24.
83. Ibid., p. 25.
84. Lillian Whaley, *Memoirs,* pp. 29 - 30.
85. So many other people were helpful in my most recent visits to San Diego: all those at the Serra Museum, Mr. and Mrs. James and June Reading at the Whaley House, Richard F. Pourade at the contemporary home of the *San Diego Union* and Richard Yale at its original site in Old Town, Dr. Ray Brandes of San Diego University, Mr. and Mrs. Joseph C. Toigo, the creator and curator of a model of Old Town San Diego in the restoration period, located in the *San Diego Union Museum,* that must be seen with knowledgeable eyes to be believed, and the list could go on.
86. Lillian Whaley, Pencil Notes, 1-4, Whaley House.
87. Kurt Baer, *Painting and Sculpture at Mission Santa Barbara* (Washington, D.C.), p. 226, n. 18. — a view contradicted by the 1844 and 1903 inventories of Mission San Luis Rey's Church and sacristy holdings and by Father Dominic Gallardo's explicit statement regarding this huge canvas's origin, aside from the photographic evidence which is itself conclusive.
88. Mission San Diego annual reports, 1777-1784, Bancroft, Cowan Collection.
89. Palóu, *Noticias,* I, p. 43, *Historical Memoirs,* I, p. 54.
90. For a discussion of such number symbolism generally or specifically in relationship to baptismal fonts even in pre-Gothic Europe, see a classic, first published at the beginning of this century, Emile Mâle, *The Gothic Image* (New York, 1972), p. 14.
91. Ezell, above in note 77.
92. For plan of Presidio, ibid., p. 7.
93. Engelhardt, *San Diego,* p. 165, n. 26.
94. F. Abbad Rios, *La Seo y El Pilár de Zaragoza* (Madrid, 1948), p. 109, and for a more detailed view of the image itself and these stars, Federico Torralba Soriano, *El Pilár de Zaragoza* (Leon, etc., 1974), p. 36.
95. *In and Out of the Old Missions* (Boston, 1905), p. 102.
96. As already discussed above, note 67.
97. Engelhardt, *San Diego,* pp. 156 - 157.
98. Ibid., p. 156. The remains of Padres Luis Jaume, Juan Figuér, and Juan Mariner were transferred from the 1780 to the new 1804 Church and "placed . . . in one and the same tomb, situated beneath the small [sanctuary] arch which is between the two [side] altars of the new church, but each in its own coffin." From this information in the register the position of each altar may be inferred, for it was also stated that "three stones [were] placed over said tomb, the one nearest to the Virgin, Our Lady of Pilár," for "Fr. Jaume; the one next to it, near the statue of San Diego," i.e., in the middle, for Fr. Mariner, and "the stone which stands most distant and faces south" for Fr. Figuér.
99. James L. Nolan, "Anglo-American Myopia and California Mission Art," *Southern California Quarterly,* LVIII, no. 3 (Fall, 1976), pp. 311 - 312.
100. According to Henry J. Downie, who acquired this statue for San Antonio Mission from Santa Barbara Mission, this San José had been taken originally from San Diego. But see Baer, *Painting and Sculpture,* p. 188, fig. 133, cat. no. S-94, who says that this "loan to Mission St. Anthony of Padua" was mentioned in the 1855 report at Santa Barbara Mission. There is reason to doubt Baer's statement, however, since this statue is not listed in any other inventory of that Mission before or since the 1855 listing, not even in the exhaustive 1858 inventory composed by the meticulous Fray Gonzalez Rubio, although there is a San José mentioned there as a part of a nativity group *(Libro de Inventarios,* p. 51 verso, SBMA) which however could not be a reference to the above statue.
101. Charles Sterling et Hélène Adhémar, *Peintures école francaise xive, xve et xvie siécles* (Musée national du Louvre, Paris: 1965) no. 91, pls. 196 - 197; Frédéric Villot, *Notice des tableaux exposés dans les galeries du musée national du Louvre, école francaise* (Paris, 1855), no. 137; Gaston Brière, Musée du Louvre, *Catalogue des peintures exposées dans les galeries, école francaise* (Paris, 1924), no. 155. Size: 1.45 x 1.42 meters (4.76' x 4.66'). For data on Piere de Jode the Elder, see F.W.H. Hollstein, *Dutch and Flemish Etchings Engravings and Woodcuts 1450-1700* sub Pieter de Jode I, p. 204. For the custom of Mexican artists making use of the best engravings on a subject available, see Tibesar, II, p. 319, where Serra is writing to the Guardian of the College of San Fernando concerning the commission of a small 1.25 vara painting of San Juan Capistrano for the mission of the same name about to be founded, "They should find a good engraving and have Páez paint it, or some other good artist."
102. Baer, *Painting and Sculpture,* p. 188. This author makes reference to the painting of the San Diego Last Judgment at Mission San Luis Rey, ibid., 226, n. 18, and recognizes that the Santa Barbara version must be a "simplified copy" of an original of the school of Murillo, p. 186. In the note on p. 226 it is stated categorically and therefore, presumably in accordance with some tradition, that "the San Luis Rey work was brought to the mission from Zacatecas," implying by this unquestionably incorrect statement that it was brought to that Mission by the Mexican fathers who joined forces with Father O'Keefe in 1892. Photo 1 was taken in 1889, clearly prior to that time, in the Adobe Chapel in Old Town, San Diego, where the back sanctuary wall of this small chapel had been modified to accept this painting, surely in 1858 when the Chapel was dedicated.
103. See note 65 above.
104. Two paintings believed to have come from San Diego Mission, according to Troy Jordan of the National Parks Service in Old Town, are now or at least were in Sacramento in the warehouse, "The Nativity," 83.375" x 38.125" and a matching "The Dream of Joseph," Photo 17, 65.375" x 38.75". A quick examination of the 1834 inventory will demonstrate that these 2.5 and 2 vara paintings respectively do not correspond to anything then at the Mission. They could not possibly have been the Purísima and San José paintings on either side of the side altar devoted to San José, for these were only one vara or 33" tall, see above, p. 25 and note 75. As for the Presidio Church where there is no surviving inventory discovered as yet, that is another matter. Also stress must be placed on the fact that these two paintings of the Purísima and San José, that of San Juan Bautista, the engravings of the Stations of the Cross, and three major statues — the large Crucifix, the San and one major statue — the San Antonio — have not been found as yet.
105. Tibesar, I, p. 187; Nolan, pp. 264 - 265 and 322 notes 5 and 6.
106. Alfred Robinson, *Life in California* (New York, 1846), p. 65.
107. Ibid., pp. 67 - 69.

108. Ibid.
109. Ibid., p. 17.
110. For references to the way a Spanish-American would see the sanctuary design in question, see discussion, chapter VI, of angels beginning on p. 69. An examination of those altarpieces in Mexico makes it clear that if such a group of archangels were in the same church with an Immaculata known to be the principal image (Zúñiga says that it was provided for the Church and later on in his letter demonstrates that it is the center of his interest, as does the honor afforded this representation of the Virgin in the community surrounding suggest its central importance), then they could be placed in only one position, above her head with Michael in the center, Gabriel to the left, and Raphael to the right.
111. Robinson, p. 67.
112. Ibid., p. 68.
113. Nolan, pp. 5 - 6 but especially note 22, p. 36.
114. San Gabriel occurs in a very limited number of Spanish texts of the *Pastores* as an "Assistant" or secondary figure to the central San Miguel but never as the protagonist alone. His appearance even in that subordinated role in California as opposed to New Mexico, Arizona, or Mexico itself is even rarer. As for the Estudillo performance seen by Robinson in 1829, there can be no doubt, an error was committed. For Robinson's probable source for this oversight, see Nolan, p. 6 and note 30, p. 37.
115. Robinson, p. 69.
116. The following was taken from a performance at San Diego directed by the son of Don José Antonio Estudillo the director of the play Robinson witnessed. The later performance conforms in every detail to the earlier one seen by Robinson.
117. Lillian Whaley, *California's Oldest Town*, pp. 34 - 35.
118. Water Colton, *Three Years in California* (New York and Cincinnati, 1850), p. 134.
119. As implied in part in note 116, almost everyone in this later production of the *Pastores* was an Estudillo which is a fact of exceptional importance for establishing a correlation between it and the earlier performance directed by Don José Antonio Estudillo seen by Robinson. For Don José Antonio was the father of Don José Maria who may have played the part of San Miguel when Robinson saw the performance, just as Don José María's son played the same part in the production participated in and described by Lillian Whaley.
120. That is, for the San Diego area specifically, but for California and the Hispanic World generally in at least 100 other Spanish versions of the play, see Nolan, pp. 37 - 38, note 34.
121. Robinson, pp. 195 - 196.
122. Ibid., pp. 80 - 81.
123. Saint Bonaventure, *The Mind's Road to God*, trans. Geoge Boas (New York, 1953), pp. 14 - 15.
124. Nolan, p. 177.
125. Ibid., p. 133.
126. Ibid., pp. 26 - 28; Joseph Smeaton Chase and Charles Francis Saunders, *The California Padres and Their Missions* (Boston and New York, 1915), pp. 271 - 276.
127. Chase, following Robinson, identified this angel incorrectly as San Gabriel but described him correctly as San Miguel, with his star-filled tunic, ibid., p. 273.
128. Ibid., pp. 27 - 274.
129. *Apocalypse*, 1, 12, 13, 16, and 20.
130. Ludovicus ad Alcasar, *Vestigatio Arcani Sensu in Apocalypsi* (Antwerp, 1614), p. 187.
131. For a further exposition of this performance of the *Pastores* at San Antonio de Padua Mission, see Nolan, "Anglo-American Myopia and California Mission Art," *Southern California Quarterly*, Spring, 1976, pp. 20 - 34.
132. *The Gothic Image* (republished in 1972, New York, from the 1913 edition then entitled *Religious Art in France of the Thirteenth Century, A Study in Mediaeval Iconography and its Sources of Inspiration*), p. 390.
133. Nolan, loc. cit., Summer 1976, pp. 174 - 176.

About the Author

James L. Nolan is a third generation Californian who has taught at the University of California, at Los Angeles, as a lecturer in English for 14 years and who is a research associate in California mission history at the Los Angeles County Museum of Natural History. He has published in depth and lectured widely especially on the subject of California mission art. His interests have defined a new approach to this subject including Spanish colonial art in general. He consciously has attempted in his work and researches to avoid the cliché of most art historians who tend to see art in a pattern of styles (classic, romanesque, churrigueresque, etc.) and has tried to understand the philosophical and behavioral use of such art in a given community. These specific interests, aside from leading him backwards in time as if through a tunnel directly to patterns of art characteristic of the formative period in the development of Western man, have forced him in typical medieval fashion to be less concerned about the artist or his style than his work of art itself and its original use and precise placement in the church and community which it served. The result of this unique approach has been fortuitous for the San Diego area: the recovery of the lost art treasures of the Mission and Presidio Churches of that metropolitan community.

Index